M000267279

With Best w to Jeff, an engineer, from a geut in the Class of January. Bill Stewart

ALCATRAZ KID

Col. W. R. Stewart, Jr., USAF (Ret.)

Published by
Crane River Press
Austin, TX

Copyright 2018 W.R. Stewart, Jr.

All rights reserved. No part of this book may be
reproduced in any form or by any electronic or
mechanical means, including information storage and
retrival systems, without permission in writing from the
publisher, except by reviewers, who may quote brief
passages in a review.

ISBN: 978-0-9995306-0-3

Library of Congress Control Number: 2018953203

Managing EEditor: Mackenzie Smith
Copy Editors: Joshua BennettWiner and Joshua Pelletier
Book and Cover Designer: Lauren V. Allen

Printed and bound in the U.S.A.
First Edition

Salute

This is a record of my life as a teenager living on Alcatraz from 1929 to 1934. My children and grandchildren have goaded me into doing this. Throughout my five years there, I was a curious, self-centered and impulsive lad who focused on whatever was going on at the moment.

I had no appreciation for the work and achievements of the West Point officers assigned there during the Army days or of what they accomplished. There were forty-five West Pointers I know of who performed duty on or about Alcatraz during the 87 years the Army ran "The Rock." Mostly Engineering officers, they were the action agents and leaders who surveyed the island, designed its fortifications, somehow got its heavy cannon up from the dock to their batteries and lived day-by-day with the wind and the tides and the fog. It was these West Pointers who lived in its Citadel and designed its existing prison. It was these West Pointers who had its top and fractured sides excavated to reshape the island from a useless sandstone hill with no redeeming features into the mystic combination of battleship and Mediterranean village that exists there today. My hat is off to them and what they went through to get it done. It is to them this narrative is dedicated.

USMA, Class of January 1943
San Antonio, TX 2016

Golden Gate National Recreation Area

The Golden Gate National Recreation Area was established in 1972 under the National Park Service. It has grown to cover more than 80,000 acres of park land, generally near the San Francisco Bay area, selected for beauty and significance. Its first opening was at Alcatraz in 1973. Since opening, the number of visitors to Alcatraz alone has grown to more than a million a year. Directors, staff and rangers have forged a heroic effort for the preservation of public lands and the publishing of their history and archeology. What a boon their work has become for all Americans. It began with Alcatraz!

A particular thanks to the Park Rangers at Alcatraz Island who have fought so hard to preserve the physical buildings, the archeology, the ecology and the history of Alcatraz. Pierre Odier deserves commendation for the vast array of facts collected for his book, "The Rock," in 1982. Michael Esslinger deserves even more recognition for his assembly of prison facts in his 2003 book, "Alcatraz." To me it has been author and retired Park Ranger, John A. Martini, who first began to tell the story of how the U. S. Army changed a useless hill into a site of national interest in "Fortress Alcatraz," first published in 1990.

Kitchen Wisdom

"It's good for a child to be a little afraid of something."

Melissa
(1970-2014)

This is a personal account of things I remember from 85 years ago as I believe them to have been. It presents my own conclusions. I have tried to be honest and accurate but this is not a documentary with citations for every fact. Researchers who are interested will dig out every error. Good luck!

Century Plants

We lived on the south end of the island with century plants growing on the slope beneath us. They were scarce and not very big, but they were blooming. (Cropped photo courtesy of Noelle Johnson, the AZ Plant Lady.)

Table of Contents

1

Welcome to The Rock

1929

Fortress Monroe

Dad was a Coast Artillery officer. The Coast Artillery Corps was a glamour pants branch in the United States Army from the Spanish-American War to World War II. The Corps no longer exists; it kind of evolved into the Army Air Defense Artillery. Dad was accepted because he was the top ROTC cadet at Penn State, finishing with the Class of 1915 with a degree in electrical engineering.

At the end of May 1929, he graduated from the Coast Artillery Field Officers Course at Fortress Monroe, Virginia. I remember listening inside the bastions of Fortress Monroe to the voting returns, by radio, of the Herbert Hoover – Al Smith election in 1928. We listened in the casement where Jefferson Davis had been imprisoned after the Civil War. The casement was identified with Jefferson Davis but hardly shown to the public in those days.

While Dad attended the Coast Artillery School, we lived in a rented home on the shoreline at nearby Hampton Roads. In front were local railroad tracks running parallel to the shore; a tired old wooden pier; and a long, gradual muddy beach sinking slowly into the bay. Clams hid in the muddy shoreline by the thousands. A sign by the pier proclaimed that the Monitor and the Merrimac fought their famous battle just off our beach.

My main memory from those days was Dad preparing a talk for his fellow officers on General "Stonewall" Jackson and his Shenandoah Valley campaigns during the Civil War. Dad practiced on me over and over. It was then I began to merge all those hateful dates, places and events into a developing interest in military history.

Coast Artillery School Commandant

The Commandant of the school in 1929 was Brigadier General Robert E. Callan, cadet number four of the 71 cadets in his USMA Class of 1896. He graduated from the University of Tennessee at the age of seventeen before entering West Point. Callan was commissioned in the Artillery and was later transferred to the Coast Artillery when it was organized in 1901. He taught mathematics to cadets at West Point.

Brigadier General Robert E. Callan, about 1929.

General Callan saw combat in the Spanish-American War and in World War I. He was promoted to major general in 1931 and retired in 1936 after 40 years service as commander of the 3rd Corps Area headquartered in Baltimore. He died in Washington, D.C. later that year. Camp Callan in San Diego was named for him in 1941. Dad was stationed at Camp Callan as a colonel from 1941 to 1944.

During his course at Fortress Monroe, Dad was promoted to major on January 21, 1929. He had been a captain for 12 years, not uncommon in those days. When the Coast Artillery School was over, Dad got orders to California. We were going to some strange place called Alcatraz, a little island in San Francisco Bay. It meant nothing to me since we had just finished a four-year tour at Fort Ruger, by the side of famous Diamond Head. We were ordered to board a US Army Transport and proceed to

San Francisco via the Panama Canal. Going up to New York to catch the boat was typical Army logic. It had a transportation port right in Hampton Roads, not 10 miles from where we had been living. But we had to go up to New York to embark from the New York Port of Embarkation in Brooklyn. And of course, our car had to be shipped on a different boat. We were ourselves assigned to travel on the USAT Chateau Thierry.

The Chateau Thierry

　　Ms. Gina Bardi of the National Park Service, San Francisco Maritime National Historical Park, provided a port card showing the Chateau Thierry departing New York on June 5, 1929. The trip was uneventful in the USAT Chateau Thierry, a 9,000-ton boat built just a few years before. It could do about fifteen knots

The USAT Chateau Thierry was built in 1919 and displaced 9,050 tons.

on a calm, good day. The Army had more ships than the Navy in those days. Wouldn't surprise me if it still does.

We went through the Panama Canal, but I was 10 years old and never saw anything. While our ship traversed Gatun Lake and the marvelous locks of the famous canal, I was down in the ship's hold the whole time, sitting on an empty Marine casket and reading a copy of Amazing Stories.

I don't remember the date we arrived in San Francisco, but the port card Ms. Gina Bardi sent me showed the Chateau Thierry docked at the Fort Mason Port of Entry on June 21, 1929. The Golden Gate Bridge in San Fransisco would not be built for another three years.

We debarked at busy, historic Fort Mason and went to the Hotel Richelieu on Van Ness Avenue in San Francisco. It turned out our quarters on Alcatraz were not yet ready so we had to make some temporary plans.

My mother, Marnie, was five months pregnant and she wanted her child to be born in the Seventh Day Adventist Hospital in Glendale, near Los Angeles. She was called "Marnie" because that was what I called her when I was a baby and tried without success to call her "Mother." She went to Glendale on the Southern Pacific Lark and took little brother, Ray, with her who was then 2-and-a-half-years-old. She thought Ray would get better care down there while she was in the hospital because her parents, Grandpa and Grandma Simpson, were there.

Grandma was a medical doctor at the Glendale Sanitarium who won her medical degree from Northwestern in 1894. Grandpa was a western hero who had single-handedly shot it out with three bank robbers in Delta, Colorado, in 1893,

killing two of them. He owned the sanitarium in Long Beach where I was born in 1919. Both of them were great positive forces in my young days.

After my brother, Stanley, was born, Dad drove down to Glendale and brought them back to San Francisco. We had a 1928 four-door Chevrolet. The rear doors in that car opened from the front instead of from the back like they do now. Because of that, we almost lost baby Ray, then 2 years old, who was nearly sucked out a back door while we were going 50 miles an hour. We were driving from Virginia up to New York to catch the boat to San Francisco.

Marnie and Ray did not arrive on Alcatraz until December of 1929, just in time for Ray's birthday and Christmas. And they brought new little brother, Stanley, with them who had been born in November and was less than one month old.

The Hotel Richelieu

I remember the Hotel Richelieu quite well. Dad and I roomed there for about a month.

It was a four-story hotel built at Van Ness and Geary with massive strength everywhere to survive monstrous earthquakes. When we arrived, it had only been 23 years since the terrible earthquake of 1906. I searched the stairs, the roof and the basement, everywhere I could manage to explore. Even at my young age I was struck by how solid and strong everything was.

There was a casino on the first floor with music and dancing. I often listened from the closest spot I could find. They

The Hotel Richelieu was built in 1909, three years after the big earthquake.

didn't have Anson Weeks, who played at the Mark Hopkins, or Ted Fio Rito, but I thought the bands they did have were very good. Everybody danced the foxtrot. I didn't see anyone dancing the Charleston.

It was summer, but San Francisco seemed cold and windy. Sweaters were handy. Big streetcars ran right in front of the hotel and took us everywhere we wanted to go till our car got there.

A month after arriving, Dad and I went down to Pier 4 at Fort Mason to move on out to Alcatraz. Dad's 1928 Chevy had come in from Virginia and was to be parked halfway up the hill at Fort Mason in a single, wooden garage.

Pier 4 was a long pier right at the foot of Van Ness Avenue. We boarded the launch to go out to Alcatraz. At the start of the pier at Fort Mason was a railroad tunnel. Coal was brought there by rail to load into barges going out to the bay islands. Just east

was the ghost of the Ghirardelli chocolate factory with a great sign on top to spell the name. It had hundreds of light bulbs, most of which were busted or missing. The huge Ghirardelli sign was never turned on while we were there. The whole Ghirardelli area was deserted. The Great Depression was in full swing.

We went out on the Alcatraz launch. It was a 55-foot boat manned by a crew of two who lived on the island. It went by many names, sometimes the "McDowell," but we simply called it the Q-55. The trip took about eight minutes, including docking. The sea breeze and the salton spray were refreshing.

Our first close view of the island featured a big, black-on-white warning sign that caught our eye. The Feds replaced it with their own, but ours was about the same size and said the same thing. I couldn't recall exactly what it said, but it was the "Welcome to The Rock" we had all been waiting for.

It gave me a strange feeling to realize I was looking at the small island I would call my home for the next five years. Neither Dad nor I said a word as we neared the island.

The Q-55 off the Alcatraz dock with Angel Island in the background, 1930.

The Q-55 had its own loading space on Pier 4 and another beside the Alcatraz dock. As this photo implies, the dock on Alcatraz was about the only place on the island where the wind didn't blow all the time. The bay water seemed quiet, but docking was unexpectedly difficult because of the constantly swirling tides. The deepest part of San Francisco Bay ran right next to Alcatraz on the San Francisco side.

I was struck by the appearance of the dock. It did not look very military. No soldiers in uniform seemed to be around.

We then approached the dock area. Our view is pictured in the image above. Some officers' quarters are up amongst the trees on the island and the handball court is just this side of the dock.

While our things were being taken up to the quarters on the parade ground, we walked up the road through the old entrance with its cannon-defended sally port. Just beyond the sally port we saw a two-story building that housed the PX, or Post Exchange, where we could buy the necessities of life — things like toothpaste, razor blades and underwear. It also had a barbershop. Downstairs was a two-lane bowling alley with a rudimentary gymnasium on the side.

Dad decided he should get a clean shave before he reported

The PX and barbershop were in the upper floor of this building just above the sally port. The building was then about 25 years old. Duckpins were just as popular as regular bowling on the two lanes in the lower floor. There were no leagues, but the alleys were kept busy. Bowling was a favorite indoor sport on Alcatraz.

in to the island commandant of the Pacific Branch, United States Army Disciplinary Barracks, which was the current name for the installation in 1929. The Commandant was Colonel G. Maury Cralle, a West Pointer from the Class of 1898 who had served in the Spanish-American war, the Philippine Insurrection and in World War I. He was an Infantry officer who had worked with soldiers as a company commander and a regimental commander.

Dad went into the barbershop wearing his uniform and took the next available chair. The barber, wearing a big white barber's apron, greeted him and asked what Dad wanted. Dad said he just wanted a good shave so he could get off on the right foot with Colonel Cralle. The barber said, "Sure. Fix you right up, Sir." He put a hot towel on dad's face for a moment, removed it and then started lathering up Dad's face with a heavily-loaded shaving brush.

Dad, always pleasant with people, started talking with the barber. Dad asked the barber how he liked working in the barbershop.

The barber told him he liked it fine. Dad asked him how long he had been barbering there. The barber said he had been doing it for nine years. While they were talking and letting the lather on Dad's face settle in, the barber took out his long razor blade, like barbers used in those days. He opened it up and started stropping it on the long leather strap to make it sharp.

Then Dad asked the barber whether he was a soldier or civil service. The barber, stropping away, told Dad he was neither one. Dad was confused and asked, "Well, then, what are you?"

Stropping away, the barber said simply, "I'm a prisoner."

That left my dad bewildered. To try to regain some control Dad asked him, "Well, what are you in for?"

The prisoner had been waiting for that opportunity a long time. He stopped stropping and tilted Dad's head back a fraction so he could begin. Then, with a grim smile, he told Dad in a matter-of-fact voice, "For slitting a man's throat!"

Dad never forgot that moment. Of course, the tale spread quickly among the prisoners and they all got a huge laugh out of it.

2

Introducing Alcatraz

The Archeology of Alcatraz

Who do you suppose were the first people to live on Alcatraz? Native Americans? There are millions of artifacts left around the San Francisco Bay area by local native tribes, but none on Alcatraz. No one wanted to live there or stay there. Curious visitors surely came and went. Fishermen may have tried their luck from the steep shores, but no one lived there.

Alcatraz had no redeeming geographic features. It had no trees. It had no grass. It had no sandy beach. It had no shoreline rocks with seals taking refuge. It had no streams. It had no springs. It had no good boat harbors. Its shoreline was mostly vertical cliffs. Strong tides flowed around it. Strong winds blew every day. It just lay in the middle of the bay like a great brown whale covered with guano.

The hill that became Alcatraz had no water and no soil. It was composed of fractious sandstone. It was dry. It had no caves. It was steep. As an island, nobody wanted it. Not the Spaniards. Not the Mexicans. Especially not the gold prospectors. Local native tribes probably justified their lack of interest by announcing that the hill (or island) was inhabited by evil spirits. Could there be any truth to that?

It's not an ancient island either. It's an archaeologically new island! As a kid, I cared less about this, but now I find it fascinating.

Archaeologists say it appeared within just the last 10,000 years. During the last ice age, glaciers covered most of the Sierras;

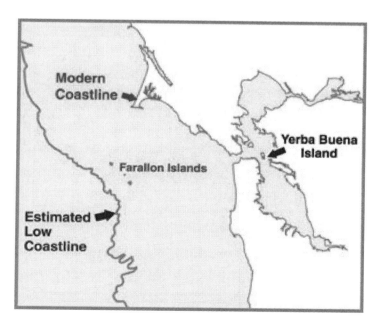

Map by CalTrans drawn for when they discussed the origin of Yerba Buena Island. Yerba Buena lies between San Francisco and Oakland, and the Bay Bridge was built through it. Yerba Buena means "Good herb," like spearmint.

San Francisco Bay was dry land. In fact, you could walk all the way out to the Farallon Islands! Archeologists say as the glaciers started melting, ocean waters rose 400 feet, flooding the bay around 5 or 10 thousand years ago. It happened about the same time the Bering land bridge from Alaska to Siberia disappeared.

So what are the archeologists telling you and me? They are telling us about the time when the pharaohs formed Egypt, Alcatraz was probably still a barren little hill in a dry valley over 30 miles from the ocean!

The Army Engineers

Fort Alcatraz was manned by Artillery units, but it was Army engineers who reshaped Alcatraz from its original shape of utter futility. There were so many West Pointers who did so much, but I want to tell you about a half dozen of them who had a major impact on The Rock.

Most folks don't realize that during the 87 years the Army ran The Rock, the island was undergoing constant change. Cannon batteries were always being relocated, redesigned and re-equipped with new cannons to improve defenses. Land was leveled or excavated to provide newer fortifications and space for new structures. A tunnel or two was bored through the sandstone to provide troop coverage under combat. A well was was dug in attempt that reached only more saltwater. Buildings were put up, torn down and replaced by new buildings as needs changed. The Army was always trying to improve the fort — along with its prisons. Fires were feared more than anything else because

Captain William H. Warner. It was about 1841 when he was promoted to 1st Lieu-
tenant. This portrait was made available courtesy of Anchor Books of Chico and
descending cousin, Phil Warner.

the only water on the island was in a cistern. Fires did destroy several buildings over the years.

Of the many West Pointers involved with Alcatraz, I must begin with Captain William H. Warner, a Topographical Engineer.

The Topographical Engineers were broken out as a separate branch of officers who surveyed the routes to the West for railroads and caravans. They existed only between the War of 1812 until the Civil War. After that, their work was absorbed back into the Corp of Engineers.

Captain William H. Warner made the first known survey of the island in May 1847. He could not recommend it for anything. He reported that it was an island comprised of crumbling sandstone, unfit for quarrying or construction.

Captain Warner was born in New York in 1812. It took him five years to get through West Point, but he graduated with the

Class of 1836. As was typical in those days, he was discharged after the Mexican War. He started a store and freight business in San Francisco. His sidekick was Lt. William Tecumseh Sherman, who was from the later West Point Class of 1840. Hired by John Sutton, Captain Warner also surveyed and first laid out the city of Sacramento.

Recalled to active duty in 1849, he was asked to find a new railroad route in Oregon through the Sierras. He was offered a military escort, but refused it to save time. As he was returning to California in September 1849, he was ambushed by Indians a few miles north-by-northwest of the point where California, Nevada and Oregon meet. He and his guide were killed. His party had to flee the superior Indian force. It has been reported his body was never recovered. The 95-mile range of mountains where that happened was named the Warner Range in his honor. He was both a proponent and a victim of the Manifest Destiny program of the 1840s and 1850s.

It turns out the first people to live on Alcatraz Island were engineers and construction workers for the United States Army! They went over by boat to work by day and return to San Francisco at night. Engineers and construction workers labored from 1853 to 1859 to level the sites for the cannon batteries. They were 40 feet above sea level to give them an advantage in height over cannons on ships. Temporary barracks built in 1854 enabled some workers to stay over on the island when they had to.

The second of the West Pointers I want to recognize had the wonderful name of Zealous B. Tower. He got the fortifications on Alcatraz started. He was the chief engineer for Alcatraz in

Major Zealous B. Tower, about 1864.

the 1850s and a West Point graduate from the Class of 1841. He graduated as the top cadet in his class.

With close guidance from the Army's Chief Engineer, Colonel Joseph Totten, a West Pointer from the Class of 1805, Lt. Tower somehow got the work going. The wind kept blowing everything around. Wages were astronomical in the middle of the California Gold Strike. Water had to be found and barged in. Everyone wanted gold; no one wanted to do construction work. He even had to bring in some workers from Hawaii!

Lt. Tower had challenges, but he got things going. Good stone for the bulwarks was hard to find. Getting cannon, mostly from the Navy, was difficult. Lt. Tower was even sued by the Pathfinder, John Fremont, who claimed he, Fremont, owned Alcatraz, not the U. S. Government; and Lt. Tower was trespassing!

By 1857, Lt. Tower had more batteries cleared and cannon mounted than all the other military posts in San Francisco put

together. In fact, Alcatraz was the only site in San Francisco Bay with permanently mounted cannon. It was also the only working fort our nation had on the entire West Coast.

Lt. Tower deserves credit. He was twice wounded in combat. For a time in 1864 he became the Superintendent of the United States Military Academy. His accomplishments made him an extraordinary figure in the Army.

In 1858, a new engineering officer reported in. He is the third West Pointer I want to recognize. Several officers were involved in the continuing fortification of the island and the construction of buildings, but Lt. James Birdseye McPherson was one of the keys. He was the top cadet in his West Point Class of 1853. He was the first Army officer, I believe, to try to live on the island. It was too much to ask of anyone, and he went back to commuting.

Major General James B. McPherson in early 1864.

Lt. McPherson was primarily responsible for grading and leveling the top of the island so the Citadel could be built up there and have troops moved in. He got this done quickly after his arrival.

His letters revealed his continuing fight to get appropriations for improvements on Fortress Alcatraz. Both he and his boss, Col Totten, had fertile minds that were always seeking better ways to fortify the island. What they wanted cost money. Congress was reluctant to give them any. They saved where they could, even manning the batteries with cannon provided by the Navy from old warships.

The letters recorded two constant, major complaints. He hated the Alcatraz wind and he wanted to get into combat. He got away to combat in 1861. He became a major general but was killed soon after by a Confederate sniper in 1864 — at the same time General Sherman fought his way to Atlanta. General McPherson became the highest-ranking Union commander to be killed in combat in the Civil War.

With the many fortifications on Alcatraz still evolving, the commander of the Department of California wanted troops on the island right away.

Our young nation was concerned about moves by the British to become stronger on the West Coast. It was concerned about aggressive Spanish actions across the vast Pacific area. It was very concerned about Russians who had established a fort on the nearby shore of California.

In December 1859, 86 soldiers of "H" Company, 3rd Infantry, took over the island. Their commander was Captain Joseph Stewart, USMA, Class of 1842. Captain Stewart was an

Lt. Col. Joseph Stewart, about 1879.

Artillery Officer. The Citadel atop Alcatraz had been prepared for them and they moved in.

It was these Army soldiers who really were the first people to live on Alcatraz. They weren't in temporary buildings. They were in a solid fort, built for them to hold and defend. They had rooms to live in, kitchens to cook in and toilet closets to use. They set up to live there and to stay there. They were doing it on orders to use Alcatraz as a fort to defend San Francisco Bay. It was the key to the defense of the West Coast for our young nation. To do it the soldiers had to live with the wind and the isolation.

They stayed busy. Cannon kept coming in. They manhandled Columbiad smoothbore cannon weighing tons up to their battery positions using Army mules, ropes and the straining backs of soldiers. When the Civil War threatened, thousands of rifles with ammunition were sent to Alcatraz for safekeeping. They had to fill the Citadel hallways with them because there was no other storage. To me, the guns of Alcatraz

were somewhat like the B-36 bombers of our Cold War days. Neither of them ever went to war, but both of them may well have helped prevent war.

3

Where We Lived

Our quarters and home for five years was a concrete-block duplex at the southeast end of the island, nearest San Francisco. It's the closest structure, the boxy building, in the front of the photo on the next page. Below and to the left was the Alcatraz foghorn. The foghorn blew often. We were close enough to hear its basic rumble between blasts, especially at night. It would start up slowly and gutturally, gradually increasing in volume and with a rising scale of notes until the mournful noise was deafening. You could hear the darn thing down on Market Street in San Francisco, a whole city and three miles away. It is amazing how we got used to it and paid little attention.

Upstairs were three bedrooms. Dad and Marnie took the master bedroom nearest to you in the photo on the next page. My brothers and I, all three of us, slept in the back bedroom nearest the parade ground. I had a bunkbed and was expected

Alcatraz, about 1930. Our quarters are at the near end of the island. The paved parade ground stretched from the building where we lived all the way to the cliff going up to the lighthouse.

to make it up every day with the "hospital corners" my mother taught me to use. The third bedroom was at the front, reserved for guests. It stayed pretty busy.

There was a large bathroom upstairs in white tile with lots of light bulbs, a big mirror and a tremendous claw-foot bathtub. It was in that bathtub I lay completely submerged when I was 14 while our prisoner houseman held a stopwatch. I was trying to set a record. He was trying to look unimpressed. I made it to three minutes and ten seconds underwater between breaths.

As a child on Oahu I had learned to swim underwater. I felt more comfortable swimming underwater than on the surface. My body floated very well about three feet down.

After the houseman clocked me, I started setting underwater records everywhere I went. I could go more than 75 feet underwater in pools. I got up to 90 feet once. It was my bid for fame. I found most everyone could care less.

The island doctor and his family lived in the other half of the house. He was Lt. Col Davis and he had a daughter about 20-years-old whom I considered pert, modern and grown up. "Cute as a bug," we used to say. I watched her ride over in our regular ferry, the MG Frank M. Coxe, with her Clara Bowe hat, her bobbed blonde hair and her stylish cigarette smoking. She never noticed me. After a year, they left and the other half of our concrete quarters lay empty for the next four years. We had a vacant set of quarters next to us for the rest of our stay.

Everyone "smoked" in the early Thirties. For the men, it was "macho." For the women, it was "style." Cigarette advertising on radio and in magazine and newspaper was overwhelming. Movie stars touted it. It is tragic how many movie stars died years too soon because of cigarettes. From Humphrey Bogart to Gypsy Rose Lee; from Gary Cooper to Betty Grable; from Paul Newman to Shirley Temple; so many were caught up in the fatal mannerism that produced lung cancer and ugly, early death.

But no one worried about that in the early Thirties. You smoked or you were an outsider. One of the favorite fables of the time was "three on a match." This came out of World War I when we had kitchen matches but no cigarette lighters. It maintained you could light a friend's cigarette with a match and get away with it. You could use the same match to light another friend's cigarette too and probably get away with that. But when you used the same match to light the cigarette for yourself, you became the third person on the match, giving the German sniper time to spot you, scope you and shoot you dead. No one lit "three on a match." But lots of people were doing twosomes. Movie stars set the style.

Curious as I was, it is amazing I stayed away from cigarettes myself. But I did.

Both sides of our building had a crawl-space attic, which was not used for anything; even storage of old clothes or furniture. There just wasn't enough room. The little crawl space will figure in a story later on.

There was a half-basement in the bottom of our quarters where the furnace was, along with a small storage room. Our prisoners considered that room their hideaway and hid in there whenever they thought they could get away with it, but Marnie kept them busy and on their toes.

The front of our quarters had a small foyer, a porch and some steps down to the ground itself. The back of our quarters

Dad, Me, Grandpa, Stanley, Marnie and Ray in 1933, the only photo that features the front entrance of our quarters I could find from our days on the island. Here it is very fuzzy; I'm sorry. The photo was taken on a rare day when the sun was shining and the wind was quiet.

Lennie Sims on the parade ground in back of our quarters.

connected to the concrete parade ground. Above is a photo from 1929 which shows it well. That is 7-year-old Lennie Sims standing there. Lennie was the son of Captain Sims. Lennie grew up to graduate from West Point in 1944. He retired as an Infantry Colonel in the Army in 1972. We met again in San Antonio in 2003 just before he died.

Captain Leonard Sims was the Captain of the Guards when we got there at Alcatraz. The Sims family lived in the Bombproof Barracks (Building 64) next to Chaplain Sliney, just above the Officers Club. Their building directly overlooked the Alcatraz dock.

Here's what the well-dressed Infantry captain wore in 1930. In the 1920s and 1930s you could tell officers a hundred yards away by their caps, their Sam Browne belts and their leather boots.

We had a wonderful view of San Francisco and the Bay. Foggy days just seemed to make the city more mysterious. We could watch major ships of the United States Navy steam right past, only 100 yards away. The deep trough right off the island was their favorite route. I clearly remember sailors lined up on aircraft carriers like the Saratoga, the Lexington and battleships like the West Virginia as they raced by, looking closely at Alcatraz and the solitary, skinny kid on the island who watched them right back.

Sometimes at night, with the scarp falling steeply to each side; with the low, wide wall edging the point; with the foghorn

San Fransisco skyline, courtesy of the Alcatraz Alumni Association.

moaning and the ancient, smooth-bore Columbiad cannon positioned in the wall, pointing right at Fort Mason; it gave the illusion I was standing at the prow of a huge, silent warship.

After the Native American occupation 35 years later, the concrete building that served as our home was so trashed it had to be demolished. There is a nice garden park there now, covering the site where our home used to be. Before that, some of the artillery batteries of Fort Alcatraz were entrenched right where our quarters were later built.

The brick wall protecting our area was about three feet tall. A fat, black smoothbore cannon was situated almost in front

of our quarters, along with an ornamental bench and a night light on a short, decorative metal pole. The path down past the lighthouse to the shoreline originated there. It was by that light and bench that I had my first real kiss. I was thirteen and the girl was one who lived in another area of the island. I didn't know it was called a "French Kiss," but I do well remember that I barely made it home, upstairs and to the bathroom before I threw up.

4

Our Life On The Rock

My Parents

My parents met in Long Beach, California, in 1917 and were wed on May 4, 1918 in Oklahoma City. Here's a photo to show how they looked then.

Dad was at Fort Sill, Oklahoma, for some extra training before going overseas to France during World War I. He was attached to the 28th Keystone Division in the AEF, running ammunition trains from French ports to combat lines.

My mother told everyone in Long Beach, California, where she lived, that she was going to visit kinfolk in Kentucky. And she did, after she got married. Her ancestors came by way of Jamestown, Kentucky. She was proud of them. I was born in Long Beach, California, while my father was in France with the AEF. I was six months old before he first saw me.

Capt. and Mrs. W. R. Stewart in 1918.

My Mother

Our family life on The Rock was mostly social. That was my mother's department. She considered servants a way of life. She had nurses and aides to help her grow up in her father's sanitarium in Long Beach. She had servants as an officer's wife on Fort Ruger, Oahu. On Alcatraz, she had prisoners for servants. She held to that culture to the day she died. For example, she kept a foot bell under the rug in the dining room. When she pressed it, the prison houseboy would appear in his starched white jacket, ready to render service as needed.

She was born Mary Agnes Simpson in a huge Seventh Day

Adventist sanitarium in Battle Creek, Michigan, on February 25, 1899. She was the youngest of three daughters and the bright one with impudence. In the picture below, she is 8 years old in her version of a nurse's uniform. She was living in the Long Beach Sanitarium which her father owned.

She was proud of her father, who remains even today the big hero in Delta, Colorado, where he shot it out with three bank robbers in 1893, killing two of them. Her mother died when she was a baby, but she was proud of her mother's father who was a county judge in Jamestown, Kentucky. She became absorbed with genealogy, searching for famous people in her ancestry.

Marnie was an excellent cook, and recognized healthy dieting years before it was generally accepted. Some of her recipes remain culinary treasures to this day.

Marnie, age eight. She was the resident mascot of the Long Beach Sanitarium.

Mary Agnes Stewart, 1924.

She was an accomplished pianist and musician, and a talented writer and composer. She loved classical music. There was always a Steinway grand piano in the living room. Too bad I couldn't read a sheet of music and hear the melody playing in my mind. I had to memorize everything. After my thirteenth birthday in 1932, she took me with her to listen to Ignacy Jan Paderewski, the Polish pianist. His piano concert was a huge success. The audience loved him. It didn't mean much to me at the time, but I can truthfully say I listened to a live performance by the Great Paderewski.

A favorite family story shows her willingness to fight for her beliefs and her determination to follow social protocol. Among other things, she was the military correspondent for the San Francisco Chronicle newspaper from 1930 to 1933.

In those days, the Army was organized geographically into nine corps areas. The Ninth Corps Area covered the western states. The commander lived in picturesque quarters at Fort Mason. The Officers Club at Fort Mason was a standout. The commander in 1932 was Major General Malin Craig who became the Army Chief of Staff in 1935 after General Douglas MacArthur left. General Craig's wife was named Genevieve but everyone called her, "Ma'am."

Mrs. Craig hosted a party for the officers' ladies of the Presidio and other military posts in San Francisco, including Angel Island. It was a prestigious and successful affair. No one noticed the staff had inadvertently overlooked the officers wives stationed on Alcatraz. Mrs. Craig had notes and photos sent to the Chronicle so they could be published in the next Sunday rotogravure section for all San Francisco society to see.

When nothing got published, Mrs. Craig called the Chronicle and asked why not. She was told that was the department of the military correspondent. She would need to check with her.

She asked, "Who is the military correspondent?" She was told, "Mrs. Mary Stewart. Here is her phone number."

Mrs. Craig asked around and found Mary Stewart was the wife of a major stationed on Alcatraz. She called Mary Stewart to demand action. No one was more surprised or chagrined than Mrs. Craig when Mrs. Stewart told her she would get coverage for her party when the ladies from Alcatraz were invited!

Marnie had an opportunity to demonstrate how Army life should be led to one of the other wives. Another major arrived on Alcatraz. Marnie mailed the wife a handwritten, carefully

worded note to welcome her aboard. She invited her to come by to visit and have tea.

The other wife thought that presumptuous. Her husband was also a major and he outranked Dad by a few files. More to the point, he was a combat-arms Cavalry officer, not a panty-waist Coast Artillery officer like Dad. Besides that he was a huge lot taller.

But the lady was curious about what life was like down there by the foghorn where the Stewarts lived, so she accepted the invitation. She probably wondered why Marnie was so precise about setting the time to show up. The date was made for exactly 1600 hours, or 4:00 p.m.

When she arrived, she was met at the door by our houseboy in his starched-white cotton uniform, then taken into the dining room where Marnie awaited. Marnie was seated at the far end of the table next to the kitchen door with her eyelashes set, her facial smoothing aids in place and an immaculate hairdo. In front of her was displayed a massive sterling silver tea service with delicate china cups, saucers, a china pitcher of warm milk, a silver sugar bowl with spoon and an exquisite china plate with slices of fresh lemon. The adjutant's wife, Mrs. Cook, was also there, along with Mrs. Thompson, the wife of the new Captain of the Guards. Marnie was smiling and cordial. She graciously discussed the weather. Then she asked the major's wife if she would like some tea. She had already asked the others. Then Mrs. Slack got the formal, full treatment. "Did she want milk with her tea? Sugar? Lemon?"

The major's wife successfully made all those decisions. She then carefully observed as Marnie selected a cup with her right

hand, placed it on a matching saucer, let go of the cup, picked up the strainer with her right hand as her left hand hoisted the silver tea pot and started pouring hot tea into her teacup through the strainer. Marnie was careful not to fill the teacup more than half full. She then added the lemon slice that her guest had wanted and officially handed her the first cup, as she was the senior lady to be waited upon.

She then served the tea for Mrs. Cook, who was the next ranking lady, adding milk in her cup before pouring her tea. Marnie explained to all that she added the milk first because it sometimes helped prevent the china teacup from cracking when the hot tea was added. Mrs. Thompson was served last.

Marnie then pressed the call button under the rug and the houseboy came in with the tray of tiny sandwiches. They were delicate circles of fresh bread cut to size, each bearing a single slice of cucumber. In the midst of the Great Depression this was quite a display.

The houseboy retired and the ladies discussed ladylike subjects for exactly 15 minutes. As the senior lady, the major's wife realized the other ladies could not leave until she left first. On her best behavior, she bade farewell to the other ladies and went back up the hill to her own quarters.

That's the way Army society was before World War II. That's the way Marnie liked to live. And since Marnie got in the first blow, the other major's wife hated her forever after.

Captain W. R Stewart, 1917.

My Father

Dad grew up in Pittsburgh. He was lucky to get to go to college. He graduated from Penn State in 1915 as the top cadet officer in the college ROTC. That won him a commission in what other branches called the "Coasting Artillery."

In 1916, he was in the first cadre of soldiers assigned to newly activated Fort MacArthur in San Pedro, California. Fort MacArthur was not named for General Douglas MacArthur, but for his father, Lt. Gen. Arthur MacArthur, whose gallantry during the Civil War earned him the Congressional Medal of Honor. It was in Long Beach he met Marnie. They were married

The Indiana displaced 3,000 tons and carried nearly 800 3rd class passengers at 12 knots in good weather. Transatlantic crossings typically took ten or eleven days in the 1880s.

in Oklahoma City as he prepared to go to France.

His father, David Stewart, entered the USA in 1887 through Philadelphia, arriving from England on the steamship Indiana. He was naturalized in 1897. David followed his own father, Robert Stewart, into the coal mines of Pennsylvania and later the steel mills around Pittsburg. David eventually settled west of Pittsburg and became Justice of the Peace for Beaver County, Pennsylvania. I went with grandpa David on his rounds one day. I was struck by the respect he was shown by everyone and the good feelings that seemed to follow him about. It is said not a single one of his decisions as Justice of the Peace was ever reversed by a superior court.

Dad's mother, Mary Jane Creighton, came to New York from North Ireland for a visit in 1885. Her older brother had to return to County Tyrone when their Dad broke his leg. She

stayed with friends in Brooklyn who taught her how to dress and eat properly. She met David when her brother married his sister in 1888. They got married in 1890. She never was naturalized — too busy raising a family. This precipitated a crisis in 1950 when she tried to visit Canada and was told she couldn't come back to the USA. Today, she would be an "illegal alien." They had four daughters when I was young. All of whom idolized me and treated me like I was the Crown Prince.

Dad was a people person. He liked to be around people. He was always ready to go visit. He liked parties and could play the piano a bit. He enjoyed getting folks around to sing a few favorite songs. He worked late when he had to, but as far as I knew, he never brought work home with him. He liked to take

David & Mary Jane Stewart in Pittsburgh, 1893. My dad sits on his Dad's lap.

Marnie with him to parties or to visit nightclubs or operas or attend symphonies, or whatever was on the program. I never heard him curse.

At five feet eight-and-one-half inches, Dad was not tall by today's standards, yet the Army viewed him as a commander and he often was. He was more considerate of his men in his day than a lot of other officers. Men liked him. He had a quality of forgiveness that was unusual for a military officer from World War I. I, myself, once watched him effectively use forgiveness as a tool to defuse a crisis and improve discipline amongst the soldiers.

Below is a photo of Dad taken in 1930 with Ray and Stanley in front of our quarters on Alcatraz. He was a 38-year-old major then and the Executive Officer for the Disciplinary Barracks

Dad with Ray and Stan by our quarters, 1930.

commander. As such, he had a most important assignment. He actually ran the prison and everything else on the island on a day-to-day basis. He dealt with everything.

Dad trained himself diligently over the years to become a master of the English language and a fine speaker. I watched him develop his card file, one for each word he added, written in his own hand with notes for each word on how to spell it, how to pronounce it and what it meant to him. He practiced using each word until he had it firmly in his mind. His choices of verbs and adjectives grew tremendously as the years rolled by. His skills helped him serve under Colonel Cralle on Alcatraz, who had similar views on how to deal with men.

Many officers and most enlisted men spent their entire careers in one regiment. When officers had to be sent on special duties such as military attachés, service schools, CCC duty, ROTC duty, etc., they were placed on a Detached Officers List (DOL) from their regiment until their return. This began to change slowly with World War II, but when we were on Alcatraz every officer there was on a Detached Officers List from his own branch of the army, like the Infantry or the Coast Artillery.

The most worn book in Dad's library was a blue-bound edition from 1906 simply called, "OFFICER'S MANUAL." It was published with the endorsement of the War Department. In 491 pages of teeny-weeny type, it detailed the precise Customs of the Service. It told officers how to dress, how to talk, how to handle extra duty, how to perform, even how to identify the parts of a horse. Lieutenants had to memorize it. Field officers enforced it. Generals expected it. It was a training manual for subalterns to use if they meant to succeed in the United States Army.

The code was rigid and Seniority ruled supreme. Calling cards, white gloves and fifteen-minute visits were inflexible. To me, Seniority, the drill ground, inspections and customs of the Service were ingredients the Army pursued to ingrain Duty into its officers and men. The Army wanted its men trained in Duty so strongly that discipline would hold up under the screaming, chaotic, fast-changing conditions so prevalent on a battlefield. They wanted to ensure orders were accepted instantly and carried out without question, even on the battlefield with shot and shell thundering and zinging everywhere while the wounded cried piteously for help.

When President Roosevelt cut the Army pay in 1933 by 10% we hardly noticed it. The $310 a month Dad was paid as a major was a dependable sum for those days. The economic benefits for him on Alcatraz were significant.

Dad enjoyed doing his own tax returns. I still have his tax return for 1933. He had a net income of $3,763.99 and a tax of $2.56. There is a moral there that I'm afraid has been forgotten. If you owe the IRS $2.56, you stay interested in how the government is spending your money. If you don't owe the government anything, you don't care how it spends its money, especially if you can get some for free.

In the 1920s Dad had the moxie to try and become a businessman. Grandpa Ray Simpson liked him. In his will, grandpa specifically stated, "In all of the years since he married my daughter, Mary Agnes, he has always treated me as an honored father and never spoken a single unkind word to me." So grandpa helped Dad construct a large rabbit hutch on grandpa's acreage in Burbank to raise rabbits. Rabbits multiply

quickly, right? Lots of little rabbits make lots of profit, right? Not for Dad. All the rabbits died of tularemia or something. That was the end of Dad's commercial career.

Both of my parents were remarkable people. They did everything they could for me back in a culture when children were meant to be "seen and not heard." They put up with a lot from me.

In summary, we were living on Alcatraz completely insulated from the Great Depression. Our home was furnished, our official travel was free, our exercise at the bowling alley was free and the movies we saw in the prison were free. There was even a prison farm on Angel Island to provide fresh vegetables and meats like squab.

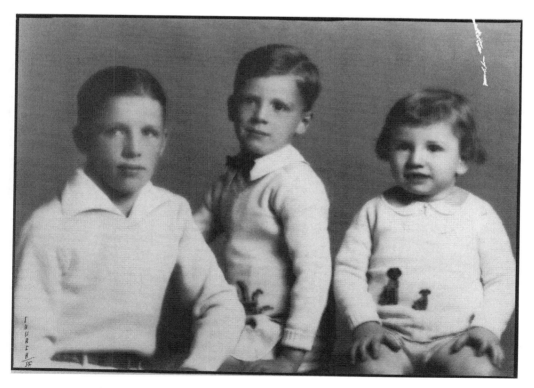

Brothers Three in San Francisco in 1930. Costuming by Marnie.

We Brothers

Ray

Ray was barely 3 years old when he got to Alcatraz. He stayed with Marnie in Burbank until Stanley was born in November 1929. All three then joined Dad and me on Alcatraz. They arrived on Ray's birthday, December 16, 1929. Ray was a precocious youngster.

Ray and Stan both adjusted quickly to being with our prisoner houseboy and prisoner cook. The prisoners were trustees who came from the prison building on their own in the

Ray in the summer of 1929 at age two.

Ray, visiting Grandpa and Grandma in Burbank, 1931.

morning to spend the day with us. They returned to their cells on their own when they were through for the day.

On the previous page is a photo of Ray taken in 1929 during those happy months he spent with Grandpa and Grandma Simpson in Burbank, California, before coming to Alcatraz. He is with the family German Police dog, Jack. Jack was a wonderful family addition and a great protector of the family children.

Ray visited grandpa and grandma near Burbank in the fall of 1929 just before he arrived on Alcatraz. He spent several

months with them. Grandpa and grandma gave him a lot of attention and affection. It was a happy time for him.

The photo on the previous page shows how much Ray grew in a couple of years.

In 1931 Ray was 5 years old. He began to go to kindergarten in San Francisco. He went to the same school I attended, so he went on the same boat with me and rode to school in the same truck with me, along with a dozen other youngsters from Alcatraz.

Ray was the only child from Alcatraz in kindergarten. He got out early at noon. The Army didn't want to send a truck up there just to pick up one child, so Marnie had to come over on the boat every day. She would get our Chevy from its garage up on the hill at Fort Mason and drive up to Pacific Heights to pick Ray up from Mrs. Krause, the principal at Grant School.

One day, she missed the boat!

Ray was out on the street waiting for her. There were no cell phones in those days. Ray waited for 30 minutes. When Marnie didn't show up, he began walking back to Fort Mason and Pier 4 by himself. Alone, in San Francisco, 5 years old. Marnie called the school, but by the time she got through and they went out to check on Ray, he had already left by himself.

He walked down Pacific Avenue for a while to see if Marnie might be coming. Then he went down steep Pierce Street to Union and headed east on Union Street. He worked his way on Union toward Van Ness until he got almost to Franklin where he ran into the Sherman Elementary School, whose teachers were looking for him. There he was spotted. The school took him in and fed him ice cream. They got word to Marnie, who had gotten

over on the next boat. She knew he was missing and was frantic with worry. By that time Marnie had the police, the MPs, the Coast Guard and the Air Corps all searching for him!

Ray had gone a mile and a third through a busy city at the age of five and gotten to within a block of Van Ness Avenue. Fort Mason and Pier 4 were just a few blocks down Van Ness. He had been on a beeline to the boat dock when he was picked up. No one could have found a more direct route. It was already evident my brother would become an inveterate traveler, always seeking the vehicle, the schedule, the route and the arrangements to engage in some new travel experience.

Ray was one smart child. He had a prodigious memory. Before we left Alcatraz, he was already memorizing the World Almanac. He could also quote batting averages and team standings for most sports — all from memory! And he updated his memory each year when the new, World Almanac came out with more figures than the last. I don't recall ever catching him in an error.

Stanley

Stan was the baby in our family on Alcatraz. He was three weeks old when he arrived with Marnie. The prisoners who staffed our household always got along fine with Ray and Stanley. My brothers appreciated the attention.

In 1932 we went to Mission Beach. Marnie was shooting for doll prizes when a shell casing flew out and hit Stanley in the eye. Chaos and consternation set in. Everyone went "bananas," as we said in those days, but the emergency doctors at Letterman

Hospital said his eye turned out OK. We were all concerned then, but now Stanley does not even remember it.

Below is a photo of Stanley in early 1930 with one of our passmen, whose name was Noble. Noble hailed from Georgia and was in his early twenties like the others.

While he was still a baby, Stanely underwent a successful emergency surgery for a strangulated hernia at Letterman General Hospital of San Fransisco performed by Chief Surgeon (Dr.) Raymond F. Metcalfe.

Colonel Metcalfe later commanded Walter Reed General Hospital in Washington, D. C. He retired as a brigadier general.

Stanley with prisoner trustee Noble, early 1930.

Brigadier General Raymond F. Metcalfe (MC).

Marnie always admired General Metcalfe and stayed in touch with him.

Our dressy photos exist because Marnie took the effort to get us nicely posed, with a camera ready and all of us in proper attire. She wanted a record of us for posterity.

Stan was still only 4 years old when we left Alcatraz. He doesn't remember much. He does recall getting stuck in a closet playing with kids in another set of quarters. But, even at age four, Stanley had already developed his own set of values and his own set of inner feelings about what is right and what is wrong in this world. Even then, he hugged those feelings to his heart and let them chart the course for his life.

Below is Stan in 1933 rendering a salute to Colonel M.A. Shockley, the commander of Letterman General Hospital in the

Presidio of San Francisco. He is dressed up, as all of us were dressed up when Marnie had her say.

Both brothers were several years behind me in age. We had little in common on Alcatraz except for family life. Both grew to

Stanley salutes the commander of Letterman General Hospital in 1933.

Here we are at Easter, 1932, in Golden Gate Park. Our parents made a point of frequently taking us to see the sights and sounds of San Francisco. We knew Golden Gate Park well. We also wandered through the de Young Museum several times. We explored as far away as Half Moon Bay.

become fine Americans and good brothers to me. I regret not being a better, closer big brother to young Ray and infant Stanley during our days on Alcatraz.

1931, Stanley enjoys his first time being on top. He got to do it a lot.

Three young Stewarts with our dad, in Marnie's selected clothing, on a visit to Golden Gate Park in 1933.

Here I was at ten years of age.

Bobby

As I Was At Ten

Since I was William R. Stewart, Jr., and Dad was called Bill;
I was called Bobby as a child. I set foot on Alcatraz as a skinny

kid of ten who was curious about everything, but absorbed only in myself. I was the only child on both sides of the family for several years and was spoiled rotten. I had received so much adulation that I was quite content with myself and had no trouble spending hours by myself doing whatever held my curiosity. I became socially mobile at an early age. I could get along with most anyone. But, I didn't let anyone get really close to me.

My interests lay in reading, stamps, seashells and toy soldiers with bright uniforms. I was polite, kind and willing to help; but I was also impulsive, self-centered and heedless. I didn't disrespect others; I just never thought of them. My world revolved around me. My self-confidence was boundless.

I was not big and tough, but I wasn't afraid either. What I should have feared or held in high regard, I learned to wall off with an armor of indifference. Many don't realize indifference is a perfect armor against emotional interest by others. If you want to block a parent, a teacher or a friend from all the things they are trying to do for you, just build a wall of indifference between you and them. I would have grown up quicker if I had been a little afraid of something, and interested enough to talk about things.

We visited Grandpa and Grandma in Burbank at least every year. This photo on the next page shows we kids got along pretty well. It also shows that Marnie was training all of us to dress up for life, not dress down.

I never analyzed what I might do with my life while I was living on Alcatraz. It was a given, since I was 3 years old, I would follow my father into the military. I was bright; and because we moved a lot I learned soon how to meet people and make

acquaintances. As we moved along, I dropped old acquaintances and made new ones. I had friends, but few for long, trading them in for new friends in new places as we moved to new stations. That remained true during my years on Alcatraz.

The complication was I accepted authority, but then figured how to get around it. So I approached the prison environment with the character of an unformed sponge.

We three boys at Fort MacArthur in 1934. None of our clothing was ever made by the prisoners.

5

Schooling

The Alcatraz Bus

When I arrived at Alcatraz there was still a mule-drawn carriage to take school kids down to the dock to catch the boat to schools in San Francisco. The same buggy would carry the kids back up to their homes when they got back on the afternoon boat. It had to go around the concrete parade ground and up the other road on the Golden Gate side of the island, past the prison exercise yard and the lighthouse. The road up past the officers' quarters above the dock was too steep. It was called the "Hack." It stopped operating a few months after I got there. After that, we just had to walk to catch the boat.

On the following page is a Sims family photo taken of its last ride. They got rid of the mules too. I wish they had kept it up.

Last ride of the "Hack," 1930.

My Attitude Toward Schools

School was not a goal for me. I set the pattern in kindergarten. I was sent to kindergarten at Fort MacArthur when I was barely 5 years old. I took it for about an hour. That was enough. I got up and went home. I didn't ask anyone. I didn't tell anyone. I just went home. Our quarters were on the post. There was consternation when I came up missing. It quieted down after they found me at home playing with my lead toy soldiers with all their fancy uniforms. I was never sent back to kindergarten.

I was never a hard-studying student who loved schooling. I was fairly smart, but danced my way all through school. Fortunately, Grandpa made me learn the multiplication tables when I was in the second grade. He would drill me. Seven times five is 35. Seven times six is 42. Seven times seven is 49. We would go over it time and time again till I got it right. Seven

times eight is 56. Then he would trick me. What is eight times seven? It took a while but I finally learned the tables and began to make my way forward in arithmetic.

Grant Grade School

School in San Francisco for me started September 1929 in the Sixth Grade at Grant Grade School in Pacific Heights. It was up on a hill close to the Presidio in a ritzy area with mansions lined up on each side of Pacific Avenue and no room for parking, even in those days. A dozen grade school students from Alcatraz would go over to Pier 4 on the Q-55 at 0700 hours (7:00 a.m.). An Army truck with a canvas top and side-row wooden seats in back took us to school, rain or shine. It was a rough ride in the Army "deuce-and-a half" truck. I'd take a box lunch for school. We took the truck back to Pier 4 after school where we would wait on the dock until the Coxe took us back to Alcatraz.

We had no athletic field so our sports were limited. Volleyball was a favorite. There were seasonal activities in baseball and swimming using other facilities. Dramatics and art were fostered. I was given the lead role in one play.

I felt I should go to school because it was part of the rewards and punishment system I accepted and lived with as a boy. But the desire to beat the system always lay in wait. In March 1932, I was in the Eighth Grade at Grant Elementary School in Pacific Heights. The following month would be my thirteenth birthday. We would graduate in less than three months and start looking forward to high school.

The school was well run. The principal, Miss Krause, was fair and understanding, but enforced the rules. Her voice was mellow; her grammar was flawless. I never saw her lose her composure, even when she suspended me.

The terrible force in that school was old Miss Belle Kincaid, the Vice Principal, who rang the bell that called us back to class from recess in the school playground. She was a tall, terrifying figure with a hawk-like face and bowlegs she hid behind full, black skirts down to her shoes. She had been teaching there for more than 30 years and took no guff from any students. There was no fun in her classes. But she had beautiful, flowing Spencerian penmanship.

I did get an occasional "A." In the Seventh Grade, I got an "A" for my project on Morning and Evening Stars for 1930. It had eighteen handwritten pages of text. It also had six pages of hand-drawn diagrams.

My Foreword is on the next page. It shows my penmanship was pretty good.

No one printed in those days. Everything was written by hand. We were all supposed to use the flowing Spencerian style of writing. We practiced the Palmer method of making "O"s on lined paper in tablets. We made "O"s by the thousands trying to get the flexible wrist movement needed to write in cursive style. The girls usually did better than the boys.

The class photo on page 62 shows that third from left in the top row was my best friend, Jack Selby. Fourth from right in the middle row of my class photo was Faye Butler, another student from Alcatraz. Bottom row, left, is Ingrid Quandt, for whom I carried a torch for years. I'm the dressy show-off seated

Foreword

I decided on this subject for Science not only because our teacher hasn't any other astronomer but because I almost love the subject.

My liking Astronomy came about in this way. When I visited my grandfather who lives in the outskirts of Los Angeles last summer, He got a telescope and we used to look through it every night I never forgot my first look at Saturn, it looked like a sombrero.

The alluring sky was too much for me; I discovered many things, among them, the fact that stars are like babies, at first

they are all alike, yet different.

My Grandfather said "The more an astronomer knows, the more questions confront him." Well--
--Adios---.

B. S.

This is the Eighth Grade Class from Grant School in San Francisco in 1932.

two right from Ingrid with the split hair and the two-tone shoes. Robert Edger at right in front attended West Point just ahead of me.

Third from right in front was smart little Seiko Yakahi. He impressed me. He made "A"s, while I made "C"s. Then he went home at night and studied Japanese. Wow! I liked him. He was a good friend who endured the Japanese-American camps of World War II.

Don't Skate On Thin Ice

My major transgression began this way; I came down with the flu, home sick in bed Thursday and Friday. I recovered over the weekend, preparing to go back to School on Monday. Then I got an idea!

Of course, I needed a written excuse from my parents to cover my absence. It was one of the rules. Marnie was writing the note early Monday morning when I asked her to make it "through Monday" instead of "to Monday." I waited till Monday morning to ask for it to put her under time pressure. She looked at me questioningly. I said, "That's the way they want it." And that's the way she put it.

For once, I had pulled one off. I had an excuse to be absent Monday because of the play on words. I kept the note in my pocket. I thought about it on the boat over and on the bus to school. I said nothing to the others.

We were early when we lined up to go into school. I looked behind me and there was my fellow student, Clarence Davenport. He looked like the best prospect around. I said to him in a low voice, "Clarence, let's play hooky." He said nothing, but didn't object. I turned around and went back out to the street.

By golly, Clarence followed me. We hurried two blocks away to be out of sight. Clarence stopped and asked, "What will we do?"

I had taken this step impulsively and without thought of consequences for me or anyone else. I said, "Let's get some girls and go ice skating."

That's what we did. He knew a girl in the eighth grade

at nearby Madison. I can't recall her name. We went to a drug store and called her. He was lucky to catch her before she left for school. She said she would get a friend and that we should come meet them on a street near their school. That's what we did.

We caught a California street car most of the way to the Madison school. We were in the depths of the Great Depression. The streetcar conductor was glad to get the five cents each we paid to ride over. He didn't worry about kids playing hooky. We could even get a transfer to another line if we needed one.

We met the girls. They went with us on another streetcar going near Sutter and Pierce where the ice skating rink was. It was called "Iceland." I knew the place well and skated there a lot. I was even on their junior ice hockey team. I still have a scar on my wrist from my youthful ice hockey days.

I had brought what change I had to pay for admission, skates and snacks for all of us. We had a fine time. We skated around. I showed off my limited skating talent.

As the world's leading authority on what happened that day I can tell you truthfully we just played hooky, nothing else. No booze. No sex play. Dope was unknown in our culture. We didn't even smoke a cigarette. We just had a lot of fun skating, laughing, ice-dancing to the music and falling down. We left in time to catch the kids letting out from school to go home. I was triumphant. I had a note in my pocket covering my absence to turn in tomorrow. I got back to school in time to mingle with the kids taking the bus back to Pier 4. I thought everything was "copacetic," or OK.

But such things are discovered. The manager of the ice skating rink knew who I was and turned me in to the school.

Mrs. Krause had to work hard to control her feelings. I had been one of her pets. She exercised her authority and I was suspended for two weeks!

I used the two weeks catching up reading some of my favorite adventure stories and looking for special-colored glass fragments deposited by time on the rocky shoreline. Dad and Marnie never punished me or said anything.

Galileo High School

I started high school in the fall of 1932 at Galileo. Several things were more interesting. It was close to Pier 4, just up at the foot of Van Ness. I could walk up there easily. No need to bus. I could get to school from the dock on my own.

It was big. Maybe over 4,000 students! That was in the morning. We were finished at noon and had to get out so they could bring in another 3,700 students from Lowell High School who went to class in the same classrooms we had used in the morning. Lowell High School was being rebuilt because it wasn't earthquake proof.

Being through at noon meant I could eat lunch at any of the fine Italian delicatessens around the North Beach area. And I could search them out on my own. The cost was usually about a quarter, so I had to find the money to live my richer life. I did it by starting to sell Argosy magazines on Alcatraz.

Argosy was a weekly magazine at that point. It cost ten cents and featured: western, science, crime and adventure fiction by some fine writers like C. S. Forester and Cornell Woolrich. I

think I got five cents for each copy I sold. I developed a client list of about twenty folks on the island, which gave me enough money to cover a couple of lunches a week.

One of my most interesting customers on the island was the lighthouse keeper, Mr. Jordan. He received letters from his family in Czechoslovakia and gave me the envelopes for my stamp collection.

At Galileo High School I was introduced to Latin. For two years, Mr. Cummings did his best to drill "Amo, Amas, Amat" into me with little success. My friend Bill Corley took to it better and left me an autograph in Latin which I still don't understand. I can not vouch for its authenticity.

The most interesting aspect of Galileo High School to me

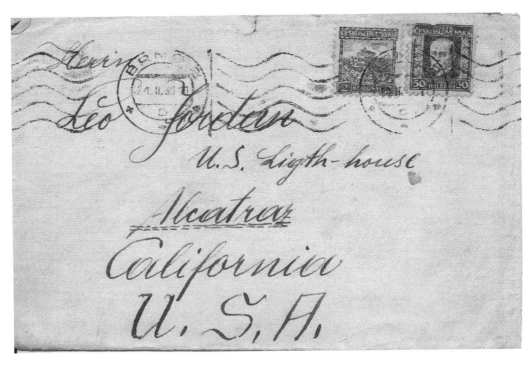

The lighthouse keeper on Alcatraz, Mr. Jordan, gave this letter to me for my stamp collection.

was the JROTC. I joined immediately. I got to wear a uniform just like regular soldiers wore. I had to wrap my legs with woolen leggings and grew to be good at it. I had the opportunity to handle the 1903 Springfield rifle. No ammo of course. No bayonet. But I had a chance to learn the manual of arms for the rifle and became good at that too. And I could wear the uniform for drills, inspections and especially at parades.

JROTC was still pretty new in 1932. It began about the time of World War I. Galileo was one of the early high schools to start it up. Our Principal, Mr. J. P. Nourse, was a solid defender of national defense and of the JROTC. Principals were selected in those days because they believed in the American Dream, not because they had a doctorate in how to become a socialist. There were several hundred students enrolled in JROTC at Galileo. It was a popular high school activity.

The instructor was a retired Army Sergeant named Malcolm Green. He couldn't get into a uniform any more, but even in civilian clothes and with a huge beer belly, he still managed to look military and to run the outfit. No one ever questioned his authority. Sergeant Green liked me well enough to sign my high school yearbook for my freshman year. I still have it. A few years later, Army JROTC units were taken over by active duty Army officers.

One of our parades was on the parade ground at the Presidio. It was a special Armistice Day celebration. We waited quite a while in formation. We rested until our turn came to fall in and march off to Pass In Review.

When we did "Eyes Right" and marched past the Reviewing Stand with all the Army officers standing up there, I noticed

some charred lumber in back of the reviewing stand. I asked around and found later it was the ruins of the quarters General Pershing's family occupied while he was off in Texas getting ready to guard the border with Mexico. His wife was the daughter of the powerful Senator Warren from Wyoming. General Pershing made arrangements to have his family move to Texas to be with him, but in August 1915 a fire broke out. He lost his wife and three daughters. Only a young son survived.

The point is, General Pershing returned to the Presidio on an inspection trip in 1922 as the Army Chief of Staff. The Reviewing Stand for him was placed where it always was – right in front of the burned quarters. The charred lumber had not been completely cleaned up. So General Pershing had to stand right in front of where his wife and daughters had died. Army procedures, once set, were not changed lightly in those days. But the Old Soldier stood there and took it. It was just about the seventh anniversary of the deadly fire.

In 1933, over 10 years later, I saw some of the charred lumber still there. Something for old timers to point out to visitors!

I really enjoyed the JROTC and was sorry to leave. I had aspirations of joining the Saber Club, which encompassed all the JROTC cadet officers. I would have had a better cap, a Sam Browne belt, leather puttees or military boots instead of wrapped woolen leggings, and a saber.

6

Reshaping The Island

The big cliff of Alcatraz running from the parade ground up to the lighthouse plays a major role in the story of my life on the island. Before I tell you about how I climbed the cliff, I should tell you how it got there. There were no real cliffs on the original island. There were some steep shorelines called "scarps," but they were just a few feet high.

The work of the Army Engineers to improve Fort Alcatraz was a continuing challenge and effort. It went on day after day, week after week, year after year for 87 years. The early results were planned by boards of Engineer officers in Washington. Actions were approved by senior officers who were West Pointers, like Colonel Totten (USMA 1805) and Colonel DeRussy (USMA 1812). I learned to swim from the shore at Fort DeRussy on Waikiki in 1925. There was no beach there then.

The biggest hurdle was getting money from Congress.

When they could get some, they improved protection of the batteries and the garrison. They put the garrison on the east side of the island where they could not be seen by enemy warships entering the Golden Gate. They created more level ground to provide a base for constructing more facilities. They raised the altitude of the batteries more and more above sea level to give the guns of Alcatraz greater range.

Major reshaping occurred during the 1870s. In 1869, work began to excavate the north side of the hill to provide for better battery placement on that end. Along the way, they studied whether bricks, concrete or rock provided the best surface to protect against enemy cannon fire. They were surprised to find regular dirt survived enemy cannon shells better than any of the harder surfaces.

The cliffs evolved as Army engineers reshaped the island to place fortifications and buildings where they were best situated. The south area was excavated in the 1870s. My guess is that it was done partly to provide the post with a real parade ground. Every Army post had to have a parade ground. The one up at the top by the Citadel was very small.

More important, they needed more level ground to build new buildings as new needs developed. And it wasn't long until they used the parade ground area to build the Upper Prison in 1900. It housed the many new prisoners coming in from the Philippine Insurrection. The Upper Prison was torn down when the big prison you see today was built in about 1912. That left the parade ground vacant again as I knew it in 1930.

And lastly, I think they wanted to raise the level of the batteries more above sea level. Batteries were originally placed

42 feet above sea level. Some were later raised to 48 feet. But this excavation provided fill to raise batteries on the south side of the island to about 60 feet above sea level.

It was a major undertaking as the photo below shows. Army prisoners were used to do the work. The major force and principal military designer behind all of this work was Colonel George H. Mendell, USMA Class of 1852. He was the third ranking cadet in his Class, which entitled him to become an officer in the topographical engineers.

Excavation of the south face of the island took about five years. It was done mostly with army prisoners. Army mules helped a lot. The photo shows how it looked close to the end of the project.

Later excavating stage of South Face, 1876.
Photo used with permission from the Bancroft Library at the University of California in Berkeley.

Colonel Mendell was in direct charge of designing fortifications on Alcatraz beginning in 1867. He was a senior member of the Army Engineer board that supervised the design of all military fortifications on the Pacific Coast until he retired in 1895. The City of San Francisco and the State of California kept him busy in retirement as a consulting engineer right up until his death in San Francisco in 1902.

Colonel George H. Mendell, about 1885.

Several buildings were erected and torn down on the parade ground over the years from 1900 to 1920, but by 1921 they had all been cleared away and the parade ground was again the bleak, flat concrete surface I knew while I was there. One of them was the Upper Prison which was built about where the tennis court was. The Upper Prison existed from 1900 to 1912 and was the place to which San Francisco prisoners were taken during the terrible earthquake of 1906. There were never any parades or ceremonies on the parade ground that I can recall while I was there.

The photo on the next page shows how the cliff looked to me in 1931 when I climbed it. The photo is from 1924 and shows the newly completed quarters for the Army Island Commandant up by the lighthouse. That same building was used as a home for the Wardens of Alcatraz during the Federal penitentiary days. The tennis court placed at the east corner of the Parade Ground was still there in 1929 when I arrived. It was never used because of the constant wind. The retaining nets for loose balls had been taken down. There had been a tennis court up by the Citadel in previous years. When the Citadel was torn down in 1908, someone probably thought it should be reborn down on the parade ground. Tradition is big in the military.

At the left you can see the quarters used in 1931 by the Sgt. Thornton family. My friend Molly Thornton lived there. The next set was the one where my friend Babe Scott lived.

The photo was taken from just about where I lived, so this is the view I saw out of my bedroom window whenever I looked at the prison and the lighthouse. The cliff seemed to me to be about 65 feet high where I climbed it, in the area between the

Thornton quarters and the lighthouse. The rock was crumbling
sandstone; even the wind could gradually whittle it away.

*A 1924 view from the Parade Ground of the main 73-foot cliff. It shows the new
Commandant's quarters just completed. Courtesy of the San Francisco History
Center, San Francisco Public Library.*

7

My Activities

What I Was Like When I Arrived

When we arrived on Alcatraz in 1929 I was a youngster stuffed full with self-confidence. During my early years I had been the only child on both sides of my family. I had two grandpas. They loved me. I had two grandmas. They loved me. Marnie had two sisters. They loved me. Dad had four sisters. They all loved me. All their friends loved me. I was surrounded with adulation. That went on for several years. I grew to feel everybody loved me.

I became content with myself. I didn't feel any need to excel. I didn't need to show I was better. I had no inbred hostility. As an Army brat, I had grown accustomed to leaving friends behind, going to new places and making new friends.

I became socially mobile at an early age. I could get along with strong, powerful characters as well as those with strange views of life. I was accepted both by those who were down on their luck and those who were filled with hate. I didn't seem to be threatening to anybody. I was willing to listen. I didn't complain; and I didn't criticize.

It didn't hurt me that others were stronger or faster. When kids chose sides for teams and I was not picked, I noticed but it didn't bother me.

I became very sure of myself and very content with who I was. I was happy to be with people. I was also happy to be alone. I was inquisitive yet I never felt left out. I could spend hours by myself reading or working with my stamp collection, never feeling alone or left out. On Alcatraz, I could be absorbed by the hour exploring the rocky shoreline and never feel the need for others.

Unnoticed by others, or even by me at that stage, was that I had developed no conscience — no internal drive that some things are bad and others are good. I had no consideration for others. I was completely self-centered. My conduct as a teenager on Alcatraz was governed by reward and punishment more than by any internal sense of what might be right and wrong.

I had a lot of contact with prisoners from day one. Up close and personal. Unsupervised. What the prisoners saw was the son of the officer running the prison. They were friendly, even respectful, and left me alone.

But there was one intriguing factor. In the deepest core of me I always wanted everyone to have a wonderful, Hollywood ending to their experiences and to their lives.

Another singular factor for me was I seemed to be immortal. Too many children are tragically confronted with death at an early age, with the attendant questions on life after death. Thoughts like that never entered my mind. I just accepted without question I would go on forever. I was an ageless Peter Pan.

Reading Was My Primary Pastime

During my years on Alcatraz what I did most was read books. The printed page was so often to me a physical treasure like no other. With it, I was a timeless captive! I wished for the thoughts, words and mental images they evoked. The words on the paper were physically mine, all mine. I could look at them and dream and think; the words would stay there and not leave me without permission for as long as I wanted them, even forever.

Dad and Marnie had a revolving bookshelf placed upstairs

My set of "Journeys Through Bookland," filled with articles and short stories I read often during my time on Alcatraz.

in the hall that had books by Robert Louis Stevenson, Edgar Rice Burroughs and L. Frank Baum. A set of ten volumes called *Journeys Through Bookland* (Sylvester, 1922) had been purchased for me. I devoured articles and short stories in those volumes from a host of distinguished authors like Lowell, Thoreau, Longfellow and Poe. There were also a lot of books by G. A. Henty. I suspect most of the books came from Dad.

So I read about Treasure Island, Tarzan and Oz. But I especially enjoyed the novels by G. A. Henty written in the 19th Century. Henty was a soldier turned journalist. He must have written a hundred novels. I read every one I could get. His adventure stories were about young men caught up in some of the terrible events of human history — usually a war or a revolution. Henty made the backgrounds in his novels as truthful as he could. I learned about the Franco-Prussian War, the Crusades, the Norman conquest of England and the fight for Scottish Independence. The youngsters who were the heroes of the novels all displayed uncommon courage and brave character in the middle of chaos.

I devoured the comics. Dick Tracy was my favorite with his relentless pursuit of criminals. I loved J. Wellington Wimpy because he could eat more hamburgers than I could. I gave up counting how many buttons popped off his shirts. The runner-up was Popeye. I don't know how Olive put up with him and all his spinach. I viewed Popeye as a salesman for the spinach company and went out of my way to avoid eating it — with or without lemon.

Reading was not just pleasant for me. The stories I read were enticing and exciting. They gave me a chance to escape from

everything real, at least mentally. It was delightful to become immersed in a fanciful tale where I could be the hero. I believe I was subconsciously reaching out to try and be like the heroic characters about whom I was reading.

With Ray and Stan sleeping in the same bedroom with me, I often did my reading at night, downstairs in the living room. I usually had some ginger ale and some saltine crackers at hand, especially if I had a cold or an upset stomach.

Being an inquisitive youngster who had few principles, I also found a copy of "Lady Chatterley's Lover" hidden in a bureau drawer in my parents bedroom. Dad and Marnie were in San Francisco at the time. To this day I don't know which of them put it there, but I have my guess. I read it from cover to cover. I found 95% of it dull and 5% fascinating. I never told them I discovered it.

Exploring The Shoreline Came Next

I spent a lot of time in the mornings exploring the western shoreline of the island facing the Golden Gate. I went in the mornings because the water was usually quieter and the wind had not yet started.

There was no beach, only rocks. But amongst the rocks I struck my gold. Over the decades, sailors threw glass bottles over the rail and into the bay. The bottles broke up and pieces of the glass moved back and forth with the tide. Many ended up on the Alcatraz shoreline nestled down between the rocks where the tide could not dislodge them.

The surfaces of the glass pieces were always frosted from moving with the tides. But when cracked open, the colors of the glass inside were sometimes remarkable. Many of the bottles had been a sturdy brown or rich green, but some of them had been bottles of exquisite Continental or mystical, Oriental colors. The pinks and yellows and lavenders and reds and purples fascinated me. One of the great regrets from my years on Alcatraz was that I didn't keep with me some samples of the beautiful colored glass shards I found there on the rocky shore.

There were no caves I ever found on the eastern shore of Alcatraz facing Berkeley. But there were a few on the western side facing the Golden Gate. They were all near where the Model Industries building was. They were all low and wide at the water line. At low tide, a sloping, rocky base worked up to the rear end and the cave was not more than ten or twenty-feet deep. The roof of the cave sloped down toward the back. There were no twists, turns or places to hide. You could count on waves battering you from head to toe when the tide came in.

At the time, I accepted them as natural caves. Now I believe they never existed at all because they weren't the native core of the island. They were in the area where landfill from excavations on the island had been dumped. The area was a shallow inlet called Pirates Cove, which had existed until fill was dumped there in the 1870s. The tides had their way, cutting into and under the landfill and tidal action, which formed the caves in the ensuing decades.

Along the west shoreline was a point where refuse was incinerated. The resulting ashes were dumped into the bay. To help the ashes get down to the water, a concrete slide had been

laid running down the face of the cliff. Going across the concrete slide at the bottom, by water's edge, was a challenge with waves coming in at random.

One day, I misjudged and a wave came in and caught me, washing me several feet out into the bay. The waves may have resulted from a passing ferry or ship. That was when I learned you ride the top of the wave into shore. You go down and grab something on the bottom to hang on to while the wave goes back out again so the wave doesn't carry you back as well. I was probably in the water of the bay for 30 seconds, but it seemed like an hour to me. I went home and changed into dry clothes. I never said anything about it.

It was a good lesson. I never forgot it. Never turn your back on the ocean. My lifelong hobby of exploring the seacoasts began then. Everything in the world comes together where the ocean meets the shoreline.

My Stamp Collection Came In Third

I received a stamp book for Christmas in 1929. It was a small one. That started it. I didn't have money to pursue it much. I could only try to get used stamps from letters, but I worked at it. Some friends and family members helped, giving me envelopes they got. I bought gauges to measure perforations and tongs to grab stamps lightly when I arranged them. I also bought plastic stamp covers, black paper backing to show them off and hinges to mount stamps into the album. I collected more and more stamps that didn't fit into my small album. I was given

a much bigger album for my 13th birthday. It was huge. I had to get a stamp catalog to price out my collection. I still remember the day I reached one thousand stamps. I felt I had become an expert in philately, if I could learn how to spell it.

The Steam Tunnel

A steam tunnel ran from the power plant along and underneath the prison, all the way to the front entrance where it went up to provide steam heating for the whole building. The tunnel was about three feet by three feet — mostly filled with a big steam pipe wrapped in asbestos. Inside the pipe was live steam.

The end going up into the prison was secured, but the start, where it went under the prison from the power plant, was, in my day, an unguarded hole. I crept into that hole and crawled that entire tunnel, working my way around the pipe as I went. It was about a 100 yards long. I liked it because it was warm and no wind blew. There wasn't much room, but it was clean of debris. There was lighting inside so it was easy to see everything.

I used to brag I could steal from one end of the island to the other and not be seen. I was talking about using the steam tunnel when I said that. I never realized that any break while I was in there would have steamed me through, and through quickly. I didn't know about asbestos then either. And I was never affected by any feeling of claustrophobia. Once again, I was lucky without even realizing it.

The Graf Zeppelin

Right after we arrived at Alcatraz, the Graf Zeppelin from Germany flew right over Alcatraz on its round-the-world flight. What a stately sight it was! It coasted through the Golden Gate with no distraction from the great bridge that had not yet been built there. It glided through the fog over the bay at about a thousand feet. We could make it out while it was still a quarter mile away, growing slowly in apparent size as it approached. The

Here is a photo from the Sims family showing how it looked to us above Colonel Cralle's quarters and the lighthouse. We liked to think it made its turn right over Alcatraz to set its course on down to Los Angeles and its next landing.

giant airship took a while to pass majestically overhead, almost silent as it moved through the fog. We had time to marvel at its striking beauty. It was one of the most beautiful and impressive objects in flight I have ever seen.

I don't recall the date, but airshipnews.net reported its route on today's Internet. It was on its leg from Tokyo to Los Angeles, passing over Alcatraz on August 25, 1929. We got to see it completing a leg of more than 5,000 miles over the open, great Pacific Ocean. It had not gone near any land since it left Tokyo.

Since its passage was on a Sunday, I was home from school and could watch the whole thing!

Roller Skates And My Box Car Racer

No one ever gave me a bicycle. Probably just as well. Back then I never even thought about motorbikes. But I did get roller skates with a little tightening key to lock them on my shoes and all.

The concrete parade ground was a wonderful place to learn how to use skates. The moves to make in roller-skating were much like those I was making for ice hockey so those muscles were developed. Babe Scott used to put it to me this way, "For skating, your ankles need to be taut; whereas for swimming they need to be loose."

I got pretty good at it, too, dancing around with clackety steps. I like to think Gene Kelly stole my thunder many years later when he did the roller-skating dance in the movie, "It's Always Fair Weather."

When the skates wouldn't lock properly onto my shoes any more, I took the rollers off and used them for my soapbox car. The idea of a Box Car Derby was already growing in Ohio.

I built my rudimentary box car with a wooden soapbox, some two-by-four lumber, roller skate wheels and ropes for steering. I'd pull it up the steep road to the Commandant's quarters and then ride it down yelling "whoopee," using my heels for brakes. I couldn't make the turn by the hospital and went straight ahead by the non-com quarters to slow down. It was a lot of fun and made a lot of racket. No one ever came out to wave me on or to stop me. Marnie complained about the cost of new shoes.

Fishing

The soldiers put fishing high on their list of island pursuits. They used the pier over by the Model Industries building by day and the pier by the main dock at night. What they mostly caught were small sharks. Fishing at night was more fun because there was a big light placed at the end of the short pier which attracted everything around. I remember soldiers gutting small sharks just off of the west side of the island. I was repelled by the appearance of the egg sacs for baby sharks because they looked like the yolks of chicken eggs streaked with ketchup.

The most enjoyment for officers and families when it came to fishing was putting out to sea in an Army Mining ship. The Ninth Corps Area had a minesweeper berthed at Fort Mason. It was a big deal to go out to the Farallone Islands, about 30

The mining of harbors and bays was a function of the Coast Artillery.

miles offshore where big ocean fish of various types made for a memorable day. The sea was usually rough and a lot of people got seasick; but the outing was important and fun.

Above is a shot of the minesweeper we went out on. Few wives went along.

The Handball Court

There was a four-wall enclosed handball court on the the south side of the dock, with wire mesh string across the ceiling and along the upper walls where the wooden siding stopped. It had lights so you could play at night. It became a favorite haunt of mine. I spent hours there alone, bouncing the small hard ball around the walls to see what trajectories it took. I didn't even have gloves to protect my hands.

On the other end of the handball court were the bins for

the coal pile. The coal was used for power. One day, Dale and I bounced up and down on the boards covering the bin. We broke the boards and fell a few feet into the heap of coal. Fortunately, neither of us was hurt much. We laughed hysterically at our dusty faces. We spent quite some time getting the coal dust off. It remained another unreported escapade.

The Crystal Radio

I got a radio crystal set for Christmas in 1931. I think it was from Grandpa Simpson. There was a small crystal set in a mount with an attached cat's whisker on a sliding arm. I would fish around with the whisker on the crystal. If I was lucky, I could pick up KTAB and hear a scratchy voice on the tiny earphones that came with the kit. I loved it and spent hours trying to find other stations. It was the one present I kind of hid from my younger brothers. I privately called my radio box the Cat's Meow. I had no perception of the explosive development of electronics that would follow during my lifetime. It was just a new toy to me in the 1930s.

Brother, Can You Spare a Dime?

April 7, 1931, fell on a Tuesday. It was my twelfth birthday! I went to school and came home on the afternoon boat. I ran into an afternoon surprise birthday party for me when I got home. It was a family affair.

The dining room had streamers. Dad and Marnie were there. Ray was there. Stanley watched from his high chair. Ray, Stan and I all enjoyed the pull out napkins that concealed popgun poppers. Marnie stepped on her buzzer under the rug and in came the houseboy in his starched white blouse with the cake and blazing candles. I blew them all out and started unwrapping presents. Presents came from the whole family, including grandpa and grandma who couldn't be there. Everything was clothing. I got a suit. I got a shirt. I got a tie. I got socks. I got garters. I got shoes. I got underwear. I got an overcoat. I got a muffler. I even got a cap. I got everything! I could tell it was good quality stuff, all picked to coordinate and go together.

After dinner, I was curious to see if everything really matched. I went upstairs to put on all my new clothes. The bedroom wouldn't work. No mirror. But there was a big mirror in the bathroom, so I dressed there.

I admired the show my new clothes put on in the bathroom mirror. By golly, they looked good. They looked so good I had to show them off to somebody. So, enclosed in all my finery, I walked up the hill to the prison entrance. Inside the lobby were several of the guards. I knew they would be there. I was counting on them. I said nothing and just meandered around the room waiting for someone to notice.

Raised up on a platform and counter-controlling access through the door into the actual cellblock was a huge sergeant. He took one look at me and announced to everyone there, "Look at this young fellow in all his fine new clothes. I can tell you one thing. He doesn't have a dime in his pockets!"

That took all the wind out of my sails. I didn't even have a

penny. The guards all laughed. I managed to keep a straight face and slowly slink out the entrance and back down the hill. I was completely deflated. How did he know? I've never been more demoralized.

Boxing Took Top Billing

In the 1930s, top sports were different from what they are now. Pro football hardly existed and few went to watch. College football was very important but with a big difference from now. In those days, students got the best seats around the 50-yard line and did card tricks at half time.

But the top sport in the 1930s was still boxing. Young men grow up now wanting to be a professional football or basketball star. Then they yearned to become a highly rated professional boxer. Role models were Jack Dempsey, Gene Tunney and Max Baer. Joe Louis was looming on the horizon.

Everywhere you looked some youngster wanted to be a boxer. On Alcatraz, it was Dale Jones. Dale was the son of an Army sergeant on the island. He was a couple of years older than me and quite a bit heavier. He enlisted in the Army at the Presidio as soon as he was 18 and boxed in the Army.

Another was Shelden Thompson, a son of the new captain in charge of the guard company. He was about my age and size. Shel was enthusiastic about everything, including starting a Sea Scout patrol on the island. Here's a shot of the two of us with his brother, Doug, taken on the Alcatraz dock in 1932 when he tried to recruit me. I didn't join.

Doug Thompson, Bobby Stewart and Shelden Thompson, 1932.

One Saturday afternoon I cut across the parade ground on my way to the bowling alley. I was lucky if I could score more than 124 for a string, but I loved to practice. It didn't cost anything and a prisoner set the pins manually. There were no machines to set pins in those days.

On my way I had to pass in front of the guard barracks. There, waiting for me, were Dale Jones and Shel Thompson. I barely got near them when Shel declared I had to surrender to him.

I told him I might surrender to Dale, but I would not surrender to him. Shel got excited and said I had to do it right then or he would make me.

No one was more surprised than me when I hauled off and punched him in the pit of his stomach as hard as I could. I weighed about 90 pounds so the blow was no shocker. But Shel fell right down on the concrete pavement, curled up in a fetal position. I took a long look at Dale. He looked at me. No one said a word.

Then I walked on down to the bowling alley to practice my game. I didn't do very well with my bowling.

The Yeast of It!

One day our cook asked me to bring him some yeast. "Sure," I said. "How much?"

"Oh, just get me a half dozen of those little one ounce packets," he said. "Here, I'll give you the money."

I thought nothing of it. I didn't know how much yeast you need to bake a cake. Marnie's birthday was coming up soon and I thought he meant to surprise her. Giving me the money was no surprise either. I knew most prisoners managed to squirrel a little money away and keep it somewhere safely hidden.

So I went by a grocery store in North Beach the next day after school, bought the yeast and carried it home in my little briefcase with no thought about it. Nobody ever checked our school briefcases. No one wore backpacks in those days. We carried our books in our hands or used a briefcase. We carried a girlfriend's books when we got a chance. When we did, we carried them in our hands.

I heard no more and forgot all about it. Marnie had her

birthday on schedule and there was some cake with candles and slices for everyone. Tasted good too – especially since it was my favorite chocolate with some vanilla ice cream on it.

About six months later the cook asked me if I would like to come with him to look up in the attic of the empty quarters next door to us. I asked why. He told me he had a surprise for me. I began to realize he was up to something on the way over. Somehow he had a key to get into the empty quarters. We went upstairs. In the bedroom closet was the opening to the little attic. He brought in a table and chair from the next room. They looked like they had been left over or forgotten by the previous family living there.

Then I thought, "but they've been gone over a year." Something is up. By that time he had me up on the table, then the chair and into the low attic. Surprise. A couple of other prisoners I didn't know were crouched up there too. I was surprised all right. There was Marnie's big, thick five-gallon ceramic bowl. It was full of some yucky smelling stuff.

They had put several of our potatoes in there along with the yeast and I don't know what else, letting it sit for six months. They had made their own home brew. They had managed to generate some alcohol.

They drank it. I left, but never said anything about it. Some got sick. Some got caught. A few ended up in solitary confinement. No one said a word about my complicity of bringing in the yeast. I used up some more of my good luck on that one.

The Cliff Hanger, or Why I Loved Ice Plant

One afternoon in the summer of 1931, I did the stupidest thing I had ever done in my whole life. It was sunny and clear. The wind was blowing as usual. School was out and I had time on my hands. I walked across the concrete parade ground toward the hill where Sergeant Thornton lived with his family. Molly Thornton was a friend and I might go visit. Maybe they would have a cold Coca Cola for me.

There was a little gully between the small hill where the Thorntons lived and the face of the big cliff going up to the lighthouse. I went part way into that gully, looked at the lower cliff and for no reason in the world started up!

I was wearing my usual corduroy pants with a shirt and a pullover wool sweater. No gloves, naturally. And of course I was wearing low, leather oxfords with leather soles and hard rubber heels! I had no equipment at all. I had no training at all. All I had was my vainglorious, thoughtless, unbounded self-confidence.

I climbed up the first 15 feet with few problems. I was standing on a sloping edge congratulating myself when I looked down. I said to myself, "Let's go back down." But I couldn't find a way!

I spent about ten minutes looking and couldn't find anything. So I swallowed my pride and cried out for help. But no one was around. I yelled, "HELP!" No one heard me. I was stuck there, part way up the cliff with no way down and no one to rescue me. Where was the cavalry riding to my rescue, bugles blowing? What I got was dead silence.

It seemed the only thing I could do was keep climbing. So I did. Inch by inch, up the crumbling sandstone. Pieces came loose in my searching fingers, rattling down to crash on the pavement below. Instinctively I did not look down. It took what seemed like hours, but was probably about 20 minutes when I managed to get up to the top. Fortunately the wind didn't start blowing harder.

Unfortunately, where I reached the top, it stuck out a bit and I had no way to climb it. The Good Lord was looking out for me. Ice plant was growing over the edge. The roots were mostly exposed, but I thought they were pretty tough. In desperation, I gave the ice plant roots and thick, fleshy leaves a try. They seemed to hold, so I trusted my life to those roots and hauled myself up and over the edge of the cliff right in front of the lighthouse. I never would have made it if I had been a husky kid who weighed more.

Still, no one saw me. I lay on the ice plant for a while to recover while I studied the lighthouse and the road between like I had never seen them before. Then I walked back down the road past the exercise yard to the parade ground and went home. I had a glass of ginger ale and went to bed, still almost catatonic from my experience. I must have used up three of my nine lives that day.

The Football Game

The few kids from Alcatraz tended to stay together. That was fine with the kids from Angel Island. There was little interaction. You might think the two groups would end up in

some dramatic confrontation. But they never did. Almost.

There was one conflict. The kids from Angel Island and the kids from Alcatraz fought it out on an imaginary gridiron field at Marina Park in 1933. Yes, an Angel Island kids team and an Alcatraz kids team played a game of football all by themselves, even though there were only seven on each team.

It just happened like topsy. I forget who challenged whom. We agreed to meet at the park by the bay on a Saturday morning when there would be fewer visitors and no school.

It was flat grass. There was enough room to mark out a full field. We marked the corners and ten-yard lines with sticks and balloons. We used string for our boundaries. We had no umpires or referees. We had no practices. It was like pickup basketball on the corner lot.

Alcatraz didn't have eleven boys so they let me bring in a friend from Galileo, Philip Caldarella. Angel Island lent us a tough young fellow named Mac. He didn't want to be on the same team with Ed Larner anyway. Somebody kept informal time for us. No rehearsals. No coaches. No helmets or pads. We had no goalposts. Few friends came to watch. Fewer gawkers. We just went at it. Those watching or passing by respected the turf we had set out for our game.

At one point I claimed their runner had stepped out of bounds. Ed said, "Horseradish!"

That was the word we used then to deny what had just been said. Now, a clean vegetarian word has been replaced by other dirtier, uglier words.

It was a long hour. Amazing no one got hurt. We fought it out to a 6-to-6 tie. It never happened again. We kids just did it

by ourselves. We walked away at the end like it was nothing. But the two groups got along a little better afterward.

The Chinatown Caper

The worst thing I did on Alcatraz started as innocent curiosity. The whole incident evolved like fire without any advance thinking.

When the bombproof barracks were built overlooking the dock on the eastern, sheltered side of the island, several feet of space was left between the island rock and the wall of the building. The space was filled with iron-grated landings and stairs with no lights. We called that area Chinatown for no reason at all. Maybe it was just that it was dark and foreboding. Few people went there below the top level.

One night I investigated the bottom level. It was dark. Only the feeble light that trickled through the grill landings and stairs, from the top level, allowed me to see at all. It was nearing midnight; no one was around.

One door was covered with an iron gate. That interested me. I decided to see if I could squeeze between the bars of the gate. I really was a skinny kid.

It took some contortions and the use of a chair I found nearby. There was little space between the gate and the door, maybe a foot or less, but I managed to squirm in. On the door was a huge manual brass lock that took a key. Recalling some talk by prisoners I had overheard, I wondered if I might be able to open the lock with a hammer and a chisel.

I squirmed my way back out, went home to our half-basement where we had some tools, found a hammer and a chisel, took them back and managed to climb back inside again. I put the edge of the chisel against the lock bar and gave it a light tap. No one was more surprised than I to see the lock pop right open!

I was filled with excitement and wonder as I opened the door, went inside and closed the door behind me. I had no thought at all about whether what I was doing was right or wrong. I just plunged ahead.

When I turned on the light, I was shocked. Arranged on the floor all over the casement room were rifles, pistols, a couple of .30 caliber machine guns, grenades and ammunition. The walls and floor were whitewashed. Everything was laid out with military precision. For several minutes I wandered around and examined carefully all the equipment.

I felt I just had to have some token of this adventure to take away with me. I didn't have a bag, so all I could grab in my hands was a Colt model 1911 .45 caliber pistol with some ammo. I stuffed a couple of grenades in my pockets. The metal grates in front were too open to let me leave anything on the surface, so I had to make two trips through the gate to take all my newfound treasures away with me. I put the tools back in our basement. I stuffed the gun, the ammo and grenades under some ice plant partway around the scarp beyond the foghorn. I felt like I had done something notable. There was no commotion. Had I actually pulled something off?

I had no idea what I would do with my stolen loot. It just lay out there, partially covered with ice plant. It was an

accomplishment of which I felt proud. When conversation at the dinner table a couple of nights later gave me a natural opening, I did mention I was pretty good at getting through tight places. No one seemed to notice my remark. It actually seemed I had gotten away with something, even though I didn't know what to do about it. I did go out a couple of times to see if the things were still where I put them and to make sure no one had found them. No one had. Fortunately it didn't rain.

During all this time, the thought never crossed my mind of how Marnie would feel if she found out what I had done. And I never considered what would happen to Dad. He would probably have been transferred away in disgrace if I was found out. His military career would have been ruined.

What I didn't know was the monthly inventory of the Armory, yes, I had invaded the Alcatraz Armory, was conducted the next day. The shortages were quickly noted and a major crisis arose. It was feared prisoners had gotten in and taken the weapons to stage a prison rebellion.

Prisoners were all taken out of their cells and searched twice. Their cells and the exercise yard were examined with a fine-tooth comb. The model Industries building got searched minutely. The gardens on Angel Island were dug up. No prisoners became stool pigeons. Dad was quietly going crazy.

On the third night Dad awoke out of a sound sleep and said, "Bobby did it!"

Subconsciously he had remembered my comment at dinner. He was so relieved he went back to sleep. He waited until I got up the next morning. I was in the bathroom brushing my teeth when he came in and asked me if I did it.

I confessed I was kind of glad it was over. He wanted to know where everything was. I got dressed and took him out to my cache in the ice plant on the hill. He picked everything up and took it away. He was so relieved I never got the whipping I so richly deserved.

I did not comprehend why at the time, but I never had the urge to brag about the Chinatown Caper. In fact, I didn't tell anyone about it for many years.

Seems to me adults were more stern in the years of my youth. I think they talked less about their misfortunes. They dressed up instead of down. They demanded higher standards. They expected more responsible conduct; yet they were more forgiving. They didn't talk about the things they forgave. I guess they were closet forgivers. I was lucky adults were more forgiving in the days when I was a teenager.

The Garbage Dump

Marnie had a thing about eating everything on your plate. "Clean your plate," she would say. "Don't leave food. Think about all the millions of starving children in China!"

I wondered briefly about how she was going to get the food left on my plate over to the starving millions in China. But then I got down to the real issue. I was on a silent teenage rebellion against all veggies. I loved hamburgers and hot dogs with ketchup and mustard. I lusted for chocolate cake, apple pie and ice cream. Chocolate milkshakes were my dream.

But peas and beets were to be avoided. Popeye was a traitor;

spinach was a throat-clogger to strangle on. Broccoli, brussels sprouts and squash were out of the question. Everybody knew if somebody tried to serve me eggplant I would bolt the family — I mean run away and leave forever, alone out in the cruel, cruel world.

I was ordered to gulp down these vegetable atrocities for the sake of my health. The idea for preparing them seemed to be that they needed boiling for 37 hours before they were slopped into a serving dish. You had to use a huge spoon to separate some of the slop from the rest and put it on your plate. Getting that mess down was a challenge I trembled to face. So in my own devious little way, I found reasons to linger after others had finished and throw these detestable mushies out the window. I had prepped the window right behind my chair so it wouldn't squeak.

This worked for several days, but then as usual my crimes were discovered. The gardener complained about the growing pile of garbage under the window. As a result, my ketchup supply was cut off until I came to my senses.

Dad rarely got into family affairs, but one night I dawdled too long for his patience over the usual peas and beets. He was irritated. After waiting a long, long time for me to get with it, he ordered in a loud voice, "Young man, you eat those peas and beets or I will pea and beet you!"

There was a long silence while he slowly realized what he had just said. Do you know, nobody laughed? Nobody! Even then, the moment was transparently hilarious. It was a family incident that had to be treasured. But Dad kept a straight face and went right on eating. Out of respect and amazement, the

rest of us said not one word and kept right on eating, each in his fashion. It was like one of those climactic moments in a silent theater when the plot is at its most critical and suddenly, with lightning and thunder, the nicest, oldest person there suddenly lets out with a horrible blast of ugly noise. I have to tell you, I couldn't bring myself to throw those particular peas and beets out the window.

How Was My Health?

Despite the wind and the foghorn, I don't feel living on Alcatraz had any bad health effects on my body. I had colds and flu. When I was twelve, I had pneumonia. I'm told my temperature got up to 107 degrees, but I don't believe it. With a high temperature, Marnie's standard treatment was the torture of heating pads plus heavy blankets and a menthol rub until my fever got high enough to break. I started sweating like I was in a steam bath. Whether it was because of Marnie's treatments or in spite of them, I'll never know. But I survived.

The list of basic remedies was: aspirin, orange juice (often freshly squeezed by Marnie) and particularly, Vicks Vaporub. Sulfa drugs were just arriving and not yet prescribed by most doctors. Penicillin was just being discovered. Its widespread use was still 10 years away.

When I was bed-ridden, I was fed milk toast and told it was a delicacy. Maybe it was. It featured a delicately poached egg on a slice of toast in a soup dish of warm milk. With a good poached egg, some fresh butter sliding glossily down the sides of the egg and a little paprika dusted on top, it went down OK.

Launching a Big Birthday

My Fifteenth birthday party was world-class. The seventh of April in 1934 fell on a Saturday, so Marnie could pull out all the stops.

I was given permission to invite fourteen friends to the party. I would make the fifteenth. I decided to invite friends from among my classmates at Galileo High School. One was my secret love, Ingrid Quandt. Another was Bill Corley, who graduated from West Point a year ahead of me. A third was my best friend, Jack Selby. Jack left Galileo the same year I did. I lost touch with him. I have always regretted that.

I was allowed to ride over in a special trip of our launch and pick them all up at Pier 4 in the afternoon. Their parents had delivered them to the dock. They were all there. My friends were thrilled at the chance to see Alcatraz. I told them about the Rock on the way over. I guided them up the road past the sally port and the PX to Building 64 where our Officers Club was located. It was at the south end next to the parade ground, one floor down. I remember it as one great big room that could be rearranged for various occasions.

In the club, there were flowers, decorations, a buffet line with too much food, a dance floor and a dance orchestra made up of prisoners. The music was pretty good too. We were all still doing the Foxtrot and the Charleston in those days. Swing music was still a couple of years ahead of us.

We danced, ate and had fun until 9 o'clock when we took the stairs back down to the dock and rode the launch back to Pier 4 where their parents were all waiting. The bay was clear

that night. A huge, harvest moon was just rising up over Mount Diablo to the east. There was no wind and the foghorn was silent. The boat trip was wonderful. I played the ukulele a little. We all sang some Bing Crosby songs. It was the most wonderful evening of all for me from the days when I lived on Alcatraz!

8

Visits To The Mainland

Going To Church

There was no real church on the island. I think a chapel was built, but I don't recall it ever in use as a church while I was there. The chaplain had services for the prisoners in a part of the prison. We could have attended them, but Marnie wanted a special church for me. She had been raised a Seventh Day Adventist. She wanted me to go to a Seventh Day Adventist church.

When I reached the age of 13, Marnie decided I could go to church in San Francisco by myself. I was to attend the Seventh Day Adventist church in San Francisco. It was located on Broderick Street.

At that age, I accepted God in all his might. I accepted his

Ten Commandments. I also accepted Jesus Christ, his teachings and his miracles. I had been trained since wet diapers in those religious precepts. I didn't question them. They were part of the rules of life I went by. No real faith on my part was involved. Belief came to me many years later.

Marnie's mother was an ardent Adventist. Her father never went to church, but he was a complete believer in Adventist theology and a practicing Christian. He gave me a fine, King James Bible when I was 12 years old. When I got around to reading it 30 years later, I found his hand-written notes in the New Testament emphasizing his own faith and hopes for me. I felt 12 inches high when I realized what I had overlooked.

Marnie was born in an Adventist sanitarium in Battle Creek, Michigan. I was born in an Adventist sanitarium in Long Beach, California. She had been raised in the Seventh Day Adventist religion. It was natural I would be as well.

So every Saturday morning I would catch the boat to San Francisco and take the streetcar up Van Ness Avenue where I transferred to the California street line. I would ride on down to Broderick where I would get off and attend the Central Seventh Day Adventist church. I went pretty regularly for several months. I would attend Sabbath School and often leave before church service started.

One Saturday, the minister's wife was teaching us Bible Study during Sabbath School. She was doing it through constant, silent tears. She didn't explain why she was crying. It was a few weeks before I found out what had happened. Her husband, our pastor, had just deserted her that day — he took a 14-year-old girl from the choir with him.

After that, my church discipline faltered. Some of the trips to San Francisco were spent looking the city over. At that stage of my life, I believed San Francisco to be the most wonderful place on the face of the earth. Just watching the people go by was fascinating. Everyone seemed to bustle with purpose. People dressed nicely. The air seemed fresh and cool. Life was bracing and seemed to hold no trace of mortality or sorrow. The air seemed clean, refreshing and full of stimulating feelings for life and action.

The LaSalle

With three growing boys, Marnie and Dad decided they needed a larger car. We had gone to Half Moon Bay, about 30 miles south of San Francisco on the coast, in our Chevy. We got a flat tire. We had to sit around for two or three hours while Dad found a man who could change the tire. It cost 50 cents. The only good thing for me was I got to have an ice-cold root beer. Boy, was that tasty.

After that, Dad and Marnie lost some confidence in our car. They traded it in on a 1932 LaSalle — made by Cadillac. The LaSalle was also a four-door sedan, but much bigger. To me, it seemed like a huge, strongly built automobile. I believe the workers at Fort Mason had to enlarge our garage on the hill to fit it all in. I couldn't wait to drive it, but Dad did all the driving while we were at Alcatraz.

On page 121, there is a photo of Ray, Stanley and me by our garage at Fort Mason where we had to garage that big car, halfway up the hill.

A 1932 LaSalle like the one my dad drove whenever we went to San Fransisco from Alcatraz.

We regularly went over to Fort Mason on Sundays, taking the car to visit places like Golden Gate Park, Sutro Baths, the de Young Museum and Mission Beach. They were all enjoyable and educational visits. The merry-go-round was lots of fun. I rode it time and time again, trying to get the brass ring from the shoot so I could get a free ride. I enjoyed the roller coasters and skating rinks at Mission Beach the most.

Dinner in the Marina

One holiday afternoon, Dad took us all over to San Francisco for dinner. We went to the Marina district, which is

Ray, Bobbie and Stanley by the Fort Mason garage, 1932.

a flat area filled in many years ago from dredging the bay. We went to a small cafeteria where we selected our dinners from a buffet line. Tipping was not required in cafeterias in those days. We all remembered the cost of that meal for the rest of our lives. Meat, vegetables, salad, dessert, water and coffee. For all five of us, Dad paid with change from his pocket. The cost was 95 cents!

Visits to Southern California

When we made a trip, it was usually to Southern California, to Burbank or Glendale, towns just north of Los Angeles. Our grandparents lived in Magnolia Park, west of Burbank. Just beyond was the town of Lankershim, named for old Colonel Lankershim who had owned the land. Grandpa got four streets there named for his three daughters and his son-in-law, Dr. Ben Grant. Only Agnes Avenue and Ben Avenue are left. But Marnie took great pride in having a street named for her. Of course, the neighborhood lost the name of Lankershim many years ago. It became the town called North Hollywood.

Grandpa slept with a pistol under his pillow. It was a leftover habit from the days when he shot it out with three members of the Hole In The Wall gang, killing two of them. It happened in Delta, Colorado, in 1893. The robbers invaded the Farmers and Merchants Bank, killing the cashier. The three bank robbers were galloping away, firing their six-shooters at grandpa from on top of their racing horses. Grandpa stood his ground in the dirt, street intersection, firing three shots from his Sharps rifle. It was a single shot rifle. He had to load each

cartridge individually.

The two he killed were father and son. The one that got away was an uncle named Tom McCarty. Tom swore he would come back and kill grandpa in revenge. Since Tom was an outlaw, no one knew where he was. Grandpa felt he needed to be ready day and night. That started his habit of keeping a pistol under his pillow.

The Sharps rifle remained his prized possession. He is in the photo below in August 1929 holding his Sharps rifle with me at his side, holding the Winchester rifle he had just given me.

Dad and I had driven down from San Francisco for a visit

Grandpa Ray Simpson and Bobby Stewart, August 1929.

with Marnie before Stanley was born. Grandpa was my hero. He encouraged me to understand and use firearms with care. At grandpa's we could see the devastation of the Great Depression all around.

The early 1930s were a time of drought and starvation. Few realized how dreary things were. Buildings were usually square and unadorned — often unpainted. Streets were covered with stringy networks of power lines. Cars were almost all painted black and had no safety belts. Men were all in gray or black suits with shirts, ties and fedora hats. Nearly all youngsters wore caps. Women wore long, dark dresses with little square hats perched on the tops of their heads. The overwhelming color was gray.

A bright spot was the repeal of Prohibition. It put a lot of gangsters out of work and showed again how difficult it is to legislate morals. One bright spot for me was Grandma. Grandma Simpson was a key person in my young life. My real grandmother died in Battle Creek, Michigan, in 1900. Dr. Abby Winegar, who got her medical degree from Northwestern in 1894, was the attending physician. Before she died, my real grandma told Grandpa to marry Dr. Winegar because she was the woman he needed to raise his three daughters.

That's what happened. Grandpa moved to California in 1902 after a fire destroyed the huge Battle Creek sanitarium. Dr. Winegar had joined the medical staff in the Seventh Day Adventist sanitarium in St. Helena. They met again and got married in San Francisco in 1903. They started a sanitarium in Long Beach, California, which had an excellent reputation. I was born there in 1919, delivered by Dr. Abby Winegar Simpson. That's right; I was delivered by my own grandma.

My favorite picture of Dr. Abigail Winegar Simpson — Pioneer Woman Doctor,
1934.

She was the grandmother I knew. Abby Winegar Simpson, M.D. was a remarkably sturdy and stable person who set a model for me in persistent strength, love without question and comfort to be with. She was a stalwart supporter of me before, during and after Alcatraz.

One Starry Night

I was visiting grandpa and grandma in the summer of 1931. One night I felt restless and got up about midnight. I left

their home and started walking down Evergreen Street. No one seemed to mind. I recalled there was a motion picture lot nearby on Hollywood Way. On impulse I decided to check it out. I made my way down to Verdugo Avenue. There was a high fence all the way around the studio area.

I examined the fencing as I continued south on Pass Avenue. Darn if I didn't run across a small drainage spot that opened a hole under the fence. I crawled through and drifted toward some buildings. There was a harvest moon so I could see clearly. No flashlight was needed.

I found myself looking at a variety of buildings with false fronts and no behinds. Even at that age I realized I was amongst a bunch of movie sets. Here was a western set with a dirt street. I could almost see the hero coming out from the swinging saloon doors, shooting his way clear. There was a hotel entrance where the ill-fated couple would probably meet. Best of all were magnificent steps all the way to heaven for the musical stars.

I climbed the stairs and viewed the lot from on high. There was a building with lights and people shooting a night scene. Should I go down? I was caught up in the wonder of it all for nearly an hour.

Too bad I didn't go a few weeks sooner. I might have gone down to the lighted studio and met Barbara Stanwyck making a movie called "Ten Cents A Dance."

I might have met Monroe Owsley as well. He was featured in the movie. Marnie always claimed Monroe was a cousin.

Then I went back down the magnificent stairs, back under the rear fence and back home. It was one of the most wondrous evenings of my young life. Classical movies were so great! We

1931 Ten Cents A Dance.
© 1931, renewed 1958 Columbia Pictures Industries, Inc.
All Rights Reserved. Courtesy of Columbia Pictures.

survived through the Great Depression with the escapism provided by those wonderful musicals. I don't know whose lot it was, but I've always thought of it as "the Columbia lot."

In The Dog House

Getting home to my bed became a challenge. Grandpa and Grandma were asleep when I got back to our family enclosure on Evergreen Street. They didn't know I was out. I figured each of them thought I was home and in bed, so they had locked up the house. I couldn't get in without making a lot of noise.

A special concern was grandpa. We had no air conditioning in those days. The day had been warm. I was sure he was sleeping

on the front porch, which had screens in place against insects but no walls. He was a light sleeper. On the porch with no enclosing walls he could hear everything.

And I knew he had a loaded PISTOL under his pillow. He would have that thing out and blasting away before he even had his eyes open. Everything was lit up like a stage by a full moon. I would be an easy target. I had to be as silent as a coyote.

The enclosure had three lots surrounded by a high fence. Evergreen Street runs roughly north-south. Grandpa and Grandma's home was at the south end. The oldest daughter, Aunt Anna Ray (who I dearly loved), lived in her own home at the north end. With her was her husband, Uncle Ben Grant, who was a leading Los Angeles medical doctor, and their two children. Their son, Bennie, was then about 7 years old. Their daughter, Virginia, was a baby who had just joined the family. She had been adopted in 1930 to take the place of an infant daughter who died within two days of her birth in 1929.

In the middle was a vacant lot used as a garden to grow corn and vegetables. It was probably meant for Marnie eventually. A plot just south of the enclosure was meant for the other daughter, Joelle.

Luckily, the gate to the Grant's home was not locked. I sneaked through it successfully, a good 100 feet from where grandpa was sleeping.

I had completely forgotten about our wonderful police dog. Fortunately, Jack gave no welcoming bark. He came out of his doghouse to check me out, but found me to be not a threat but one of his charges to guard and protect. So he went to a spot in the garden he had hollowed out for his own comfort. He lay

there to watch out for me and see I was OK. My luck was holding.

I crept around to the back of Aunt Anna Ray's home. No one noticed. Good. In her backyard was a swing with an awning cover. Looked good to me. I could at least get a nap there.

Wrong. The night had turned cold. The sky was clear. The wind had gone dead calm. The temperature dropped like a rock. It was too cold in the hammock to do anything but shiver. I had to get warmer.

No problem. There was an array of clotheslines in her backyard with bundles of sheets and towels hung out on clothespins to dry. Fresh, clean sheets. Dry to the touch! I grabbed some and rolled up in them on the hammock.

They did no good. Cold air seeped up from the bottom of the hammock and oozed right through my sheets. I still shivered.

So I went over to Jack and asked him to move away so I could lie on the ground in the hollow he had just warmed. By golly, he did. I lay on the ground wrapped again in sheets from the clotheslines.

That didn't work either. I still shivered. It got worse as the ground beneath me grew cooler.

In desperation, I looked at Jack's doghouse. It was big enough for me. It had a wooden floor over the dirt. It had sides. It had a roof. It was big enough for me to crawl in. I got some added bath towels from the lines and squirmed my way inside. This time, on impulse, I put all the sheets under me instead of on top. I used the sheets along with most of the bath towels, saving one bath towel for a pillow and the other for cover. That's when I learned you stay warm by putting the good insulation underneath, not on top. The doghouse seemed much cleaner

than I thought it would be. It was quite comfortable. It soon got warm enough that I could get in some needed sleep.

When it seemed about 5:00 a.m., I got up, replaced the sheets on the clotheslines as best I could, went over to Grandma's window and tapped to get her attention. She always got up around 5:00 a.m. She did that day too. She heard me at the window, came over and looked. When she saw it was me, she got excited and told me to come in by the back kitchen door. By the time I got there she had it unlocked and open. I got a warm welcome and a quick demand to tell her what had happened.

As soon as I finished, she went to the front porch and got Grandpa. He came back, pulling on his suspenders and slippers. I had to tell him the whole story again.

Neither one scolded me. They were both happy I was back inside the house and OK. Both apologized for locking me out — unintentionally. Not a word about how the whole thing was really my fault.

The next thing Grandpa told me was astounding. "Bobby", he said, "I let that doghouse get dirtier and dirtier for years. It was really filthy. Yesterday, I got a feeling I should clean it up. So yesterday, I got out the big hose and a scrub brush and soap and gave Jack's doghouse a much needed cleaning. The Lord made me do it so I could prepare it for you to sleep there!"

Yosemite

In the spring of 1934, Dad took me with him to visit Yosemite. We were to go back the same day, but we ran into

friends. He agreed I could stay with them for a week. Wow!

I watched the spectacular, nightly firefalls and went on exploratory adventures up in the mountains surrounding the valley. It was a perfect vacation for a teenager. Of course, I had to add to the suspense by disappearing above Yosemite Falls with the 14-year-old daughter of my host family. Actually, I was on my best behavior and it was a pleasant memory for both of us — especially dipping our feet in the pool just at the head of Yosemite Falls. From where we were, we had a great view of the half-mile drop of the water to the valley floor!

9

Pier 4

The USAT General Frank M. Coxe

Our regular transport was named the Major General Frank M. Coxe. It went to Angel Island as well as Alcatraz. We just called it the Coxe. No one ever asked who General Coxe was. No one cared. Being curious, I dug out some facts on the man.

He was born in Philadelphia, Pennsylvania, in 1842. By 1860 he was working as a clerk in Philadelphia. In 1863, during the Civil War, he volunteered to join the 87th US Infantry regiment from Pennsylvania. He was taken in as a 2nd Lt. He was promoted to 1st Lt. in 1864, and Captain in 1865. His regiment was in constant battle during Sheridan's Shenandoah campaign, the bitter Battle of the Wilderness and the Siege of Petersburg. The 87th was at Appomattox Court House for General Lee's

The Major General Frank M. Coxe was built for the Army in 1922 to provide military ferry services within San Francisco Bay. It was 144-feet long and looked just like the ship in the movie, "The African Queen," used by the Germans to patrol Lake Tanganyika in World War I.

surrender. At war's end, Frank Coxe was a Brevet Colonel. He was mustered out, but returned as a Captain. He rose in rank as a Paymaster.

By 1900, he was a Colonel and Paymaster for the entire Pacific District of the U.S. Army. He was promoted to Brigadier General in 1904 and retired. In declining health, he and his wife, Ella, lived in a rented home just outside the gate to the Presidio of San Francisco where they could get medical help from Letterman Army Hospital. He died in 1916, shortly after the death of his wife. He evidently received a tombstone promotion to Major General. "Tombstone promotions" used to be given occasionally to Army, Navy and Marine officers when they died. It didn't happen often in the Army.

He was transparently an officer who was respected and trusted. He met all his obligations to his wife, to the United

States Army and to his country. As kids, we never cared who he was. He deserved our respect but we ignored him.

Security

The only boats normally permitted to dock at Pier 4 were the USAT Coxe and the Alcatraz launch. The Coxe provided ferry service to both Alcatraz and to Angel Island. Our own launch went only to Alcatraz. The only folks transported were those who lived on Angel Island or Alcatraz, and their guests. Water barges were the only other traffic to Alcatraz. Alcatraz had no water of its own.

From Alcatraz, we school kids caught the launch which left at 0700 hours. We usually returned on the Coxe on its afternoon schedule. It was mostly the same folks using the same schedules every day. Everyone got to know who was who. One of the young girls from Angel Island was named Mifawny Stetson. She was called "My Fanny" a lot. Poor girl. Kids are often cruel. She suffered.

There was a long pier out to the dock that we usually had to walk. Vehicles were rarely allowed to come out to the dock. The boat crews could recognize most folks, except for guests, so there were no badges and no ID checks. We just got on board as we arrived. No lines.

There was no evident security, but the dock remained remarkably free of any security challenges. There was usually a crewman stationed at the start of the gangplank, but I never noticed him challenge anyone. I sensed he knew everyone and was observant.

We kids never thought about security. We did not have backpacks in those days. We carried our books and papers loose in our hands or we had a briefcase. We could have carried anything in those briefcases. They were never searched. I carried a lunchbox and added a briefcase in high school.

The Crew of the Coxe

The crew of the Coxe lived aboard the boat. They had crew quarters below deck, forward of the cargo hatch.

We never thought about them. They were just part of the background. What we never realized was that they ate aboard too. They had a wonderful cook who prepared scrumptious food. Meals for those hard-working seamen often consisted of huge baked potatoes with all the trimmings, salads, choice New York steaks, apple pie and ice cream. With the Great Depression all around them, they took care to have their meals when they were berthed at Pier 4 during times when no one was around. The crew never talked about what a good deal they had. Turnover was very low.

The Dock Master

There was a one-room shack at the end of the dock. An old Army sergeant named Davis ran it. I don't ever recall any challenges to his authority. He was a thin, trim, quiet soldier who always wore his khaki uniform with blouse and high collar.

When he went outside the shack, his Army cap was always on at a correct angle. I never saw him smoking, taking a drink or fraternizing with anyone.

He didn't invite us into his office, but he never denied us entrance either. His office had a government desk, a phone and two or three chairs plus a file cabinet. His desk was always cluttered with a lot of paper. His typewriter got a lot of use.

The most interesting details were on his inside walls. They were literally covered with full black and white publicity photos of an attractive young lady. He let it be known the photos were of his daughter who was a movie starlet in Hollywood. I came away with the impression it was Toby Wing, but it wasn't. When I questioned my Dad, he said it was Jean Parker.

But it wasn't her either. The quiet sergeant had fooled us

Jean Parker starred in movies in the 1920's and 1930's.

all through the years he was there. No one ever doubted him. We were just happy for him to have such a beautiful daughter, and to bask in the nearness of a Hollywood personality.

The Dock Fight

There was one hell of a fight one day in 1932, right on the dock, close to Sergeant Davis's shed. It was in the afternoon. We were waiting for the Coxe to leave and take us all back home from school. The two boys who fought were about fifteen. Both were from Angel Island. Both were the sons of officers stationed at Fort McDowell. I had not noticed any friction between them.

One was Ed Larner. He seemed like he would be a bully, but he never pushed it much. I just sensed it about him. His Dad was the Quartermaster at Fort McDowell, Captain William Larner. Captain Larner and his wife, Grace, doted on their only son, Edward, who was born in 1917. At the age of fifteen in 1932, Ed was a heavy-set youngster of hard fat. He was about 210 pounds of impulsive, happy-go-lucky, cocksure teenager.

The other was Mac McMurdo. The doctor at Fort McDowell was Major Hew McMurdo. He and his wife, Dahlia, had three children, the middle being a son named Hew McMurdo, Jr. Hew, Jr., called Mac, was born in Australia in 1917. In 1932, he was a strong, quiet lad of fifteen with big bones. He probably already weighed about 170 pounds.

There was no preliminary name-calling or incident. No referee and no bell. All of a sudden they were standing there slugging at each other. I have never seen another fight like it. It

went on for what seemed like a very long time — probably really four or five minutes. No one stopped them. They just whaled away.

What I still remember vividly were the expressions on their faces. Their faces were both set in an intent and focused way; yet they had almost dreamy expressions as if they were doing something they really wanted to do, not enjoying it but wanting to experience it. I have never forgotten the looks on their faces; their expressions were so alike.

It was the most ferocious fight I have ever seen. The two youngsters slugged it out, toe-to-toe, incessantly hammering and battering each other without any stop. They quit only when they had to catch the ferry home.

It was a bloody draw. No one interfered, certainly not a 13-year-old skinny kid of maybe 95-pounds like me. I still remember that spectacular fight partly because both boys were lost in World War II 10 years later.

Private Hew McMurdo, Jr. enlisted in the Army in 1937. He was assigned to the 31st Infantry Regiment in the Philippines. He was among those who battled the Japanese. He was captured with the fall of Bataan. He survived the Bataan Death March, but died at the terrible Cabanatuan prison in Luzon in October 1942 — just 25 years old.

Ed Larner became an Aviation Cadet. He won his wings in the Army Air Corps. He became a B-25 combat pilot, distinguished in combat against Japanese. He commanded the 90th Squadron of the third Attack Group when he was killed in a plane crash in April 1943 — just 26 years old. He was already a major.

I remember that fight like it was yesterday because of the looks on the faces of both boys and because of what happened to them both in World War II.

10

Building the Prison

The Army Mission for Fort Alcatraz changed in 1907. There had been prisoners around Alcatraz over the years since 1859, but it had basically been a fort defending San Francisco.

With all the soldiers in the Philippines after the Philippine Insurrection, several got into trouble. They received prison sentences. Rather than send them all the way back to Fort Leavenworth, the Army started dropping more off at Alcatraz. To accommodate them, a larger prison was needed.

Major Rueben B. Turner, West Point Class of 1881, met the challenge, even though he was a Constructing Quartermaster, not an Engineer. I want to recognize his accomplishments at Alcatraz from 1907 to 1912.

He was not a distinguished cadet in his Class, graduating number 19 out of 53 cadets in his Class. He started as an Infantry officer, but his talents with mathematics and construction

Major Reuben B. Turner, about 1895.

became known. Beginning in 1892, he started being detached from the 6th Infantry to run construction projects at various Army posts. He became known as a Constructing Quartermaster.

As we specialize more and more, it is easy to forget that officers in the U.S. Army in those days, a century ago, were expected to be able do anything, anywhere, anytime. They might be drilling troops one day and act as a diplomatic attaché the next. They could recruit reservists one day and be running forestry camps the next. Here we have the case of a trained Infantry officer assigned to Quartermaster duties, now charged with constructing a major new prison for convicts.

Building the New Prison

There were several buildings used as prisons throughout the history of Fort Alcatraz. In 1907, Alcatraz was redesignated

from an Army Fort to a Military Prison. Major Turner was assigned as the first Commandant of the Military Prison. Part of his mission was to build a new prison able to handle all of the Army convicts that might be sent there. There had been several buildings used as prisons over the years and others built as temporary prisons. They were all too small, too old and too outmoded for what the Army wanted in 1907.

Major Turner received very little money to do anything. With only $250,000 he built the famous prison you see today. It took six years. It was labeled the largest, reinforced concrete building in the world for 30 years until the Pentagon was built in Washington, D.C. The Pentagon opened in January 1943.

First he tore down the old military citadel from 1859. He saved what he could. He reused part of it for design. He saved the moat and bottom area to be used as dungeons for the new cell house.

It is fabled that Major Turner used salt water in the cement and that is why it deteriorated. However, records show he brought fresh water in and used fresh water in his concrete throughout the construction. He had some of his prisoners quarrying rock from nearby Angel Island. He had other prisoners clearing land, constructing cement walls, setting iron bars in place and laying electric lines. He built 600 individual cells for 600 individual prisoners, which was unheard of in those days. Flushometer toilets were installed in each cell to provide flushing water for each prisoner, but no water tank was left within the cell, which might be used by the prisoner for any nefarious purpose.

Amidst all this shuffling and moving and work detailing of prisoners, it is amazing to me that I could find no record of

any attempted escape by prisoners during the entire six years it took to complete the construction. Were they just not reported? Did the prisoners feel the new prison would be so much better than the one in which they were incarcerated that they would do everything to make it happen?

How would you have felt as a prisoner to be working on the new cell house knowing when it was finished you would be locked up in one of its cells?

What Major Turner accomplished in those days for $250,000 ranks to me as one of the top construction successes of the century.

Rainwater Harvesting

I have wondered for years why rain water was not harvested on Alcatraz. From the start in the 1850s, water was barged in by the Army and pumped up by the barge pumps to cisterns in various places. Several new cisterns were designed to be part of the water supply for the new prison building starting in 1907. They were placed on the roof of the new prison by 1912. The water for the new cisterns continued to be supplied by barges. I know of no attempt by the Army to replace this with any island sufficient resource. Maybe the Army had little faith in water pumps in those days. After all, they didn't use any water pumps when they built the Panama Canal.

I believe the Federal Bureau of Prisons tried to dig a water well on The Rock with no results. I note they also built a water tower. But I've found no mention of any attempt to establish

a rainwater catchment system right on Alcatraz to harvest rainwater as a source of supply.

Rain does fall every year on Alcatraz. I've not seen any figures for the island itself, but there are figures for San Francisco. They indicate that average rainfalls for San Francisco for the years when the new prison was being built was around 19 inches a year. San Francisco rainfall for the last century has averaged 22 inches a year. The lowest annual rainfall for San Francisco was 1975 when it received only eight inches of rain. The highest year was 1997 when San Francisco had 47 inches of rain. So there was rainfall on Alcatraz.

The roof of the new prison was about 40,000-square-feet. Rainwater catchment could have been 80,000-cubic-feet a year, or over 5 million gallons of water. Looks to me like a rainwater catchment system could have provided enough water for the island all year long.

Rainwater catchment was not unheard of, even in the 1850s. Bermuda had already been doing it for a couple of hundred years. But it is only fair to report activity on Bermuda was essentially individual. The Bermuda government didn't officially approve the technique and require action until the 1930s. In addition, Major Turner may have considered rainwater, but decided he didn't know how to treat water effectively to keep it healthy to drink.

But it is interesting I found no record of anyone considering rainwater as a source for water on Alcatraz. If they had, the history of Alcatraz might well have been different.

11

The Army Prisoners

The Commandant's View

When we arrived on Alcatraz in 1929, the Commandant of the Pacific Branch, US Disciplinary Barracks, was Colonel G. Maury Cralle, a graduate of West Point from the Class of 1898. He was what is known amongst cadets as a "Goat." The top cadets were called "Engineers" and the bottom cadets were called "Goats." Cadet Cralle was definitely a "Goat." He graduated number 56 in a class of 59. He was almost the bottom-ranking cadet in his class. But that didn't disturb him. He served his country well through the Spanish-American War and the Philippine Insurrection as an Infantry officer. The lower ranking cadets in classes from West Point have often become

Captain G. Maury Cralle, USMA 1896, as he looked in 1917. The photo comes courtesy of his grandson, LTC Maury S. Cralle, Jr., USMA 1956.

very effective combat leaders in war. His contribution to Alcatraz history is noteworthy.

He took charge of Alcatraz in 1926, three years before we arrived, and immediately ran into a hornet's nest. No prisoners had been able to escape for many years. Discontent had risen to the level where prisoners were planning to make a total mass break. On signal, every prisoner was to rush to the shore, jump in and start swimming. Sure, many would drown, but some had to be able to escape. They thought.

Colonel Cralle found out about the plan and his treatment became a case study in effective leadership. Instead of doubling guards and punishing prisoners, he called them all together on the windy, concrete parade ground. No guards had weapons. By himself, unarmed, he marched to the front of the mob and told them he knew of their plot.

Major W.R. Stewart, Executive Officer, Pacific Branch, USDB, 1932.

He recounted for them the stupidity of jumping in the cold bay waters and drowning by the score. He told them about the huge tidal currents with water all the way from Sacramento to San Jose that flowed in and out of the Golden Gate, at their worst rushing by Alcatraz. He told them about the likelihood of ferocious sharks in the ocean and bay waters. He told them they were better off in prison than out trying to live during the Great Depression with huge unemployment rates. Then he told them he wouldn't stop them. Neither he nor the guards would sound any alarms. They could start jumping in any time they wanted to. He wouldn't even call the cops!

Well, this so disarmed the prisoners that they lost their enthusiasm for the mass break. They talked amongst themselves. Slowly some, then all, began drifting back up the hill to the prison and their cells. What Colonel Cralle succeeded in doing was remarkable. It averted a mass disaster. It outshone most Hollywood fantasies.

To tell you the truth, I never met Colonel Cralle. But I sure admire him.

The Executive Officer's View

My Dad was Executive Officer of Alcatraz for five years. From 1929 to 1934, he was in direct charge of all the prisoners and all the guards and all other activities on the island. He was on the spot twenty-four hours a day, seven days a week. To me, he is the world's greatest authority on the prisoners of Alcatraz during the early 1930s.

In 1930, for a program about boxing matches between prisoners held at Fort Mason, he wrote an article about his prisoners that I believe is the most realistic record available of what the life of an Army prisoner was like in those days. He had been in that duty for a year when he wrote it and had gained the experience needed to describe what went on.

Here is what he had to say in 1930, reprinted from an Alcatraz boxing match program at Fort Mason. You will see the cover page of that program later on. See the section in this chapter titled "The Chaplain's View."

"The United States Disciplinary Barracks are the penitentiaries of the United States Army. In them are confined military personnel sentenced under military law to dishonorable discharge and confinement at hard labor for periods of six months or longer.

Military law is that branch of law which regulates the military establishment. It is based on the Articles of War promulgated by Congress for the government of the Armies of the United States. These articles, at present 121 in number, cover not only military offenses, such as desertion, disobedience of orders, mutiny, etc., but also offenses against the civil law. Hence any person in the military service may be tried under Military Law for manslaughter, burglary, embezzlement, assault or similar crimes as well as for purely military offenses.

The United States Disciplinary Barracks formerly consisted of the main barracks at Fort Leavenworth, Kansas, having a capacity of 2400 prisoners, with two branches,

the Atlantic Branch, in New York, and the Pacific Branch, in San Francisco. However, in 1929, in order to help alleviate the overcrowding of Federal Penitentiaries, the Disciplinary Barracks at Fort Leavenworth, Kansas, were transferred to the Department of Justice, leaving only the two branches to function as Army Prisons. Since then military offenders from Army posts East of the Mississippi River have been confined at the Atlantic Branch, while those from widely scattered Army stations from the Mississippi River westward to Hawaii, the Philippine Islands and China and from Alaska south to Panama are confined at the Pacific Branch in San Francisco.

The mission of the United States Disciplinary Barracks is two-fold – first, rehabilitation, and second, punitive. Punishment by confinement at hard labor is not the paramount aim of such institutions. The reclamation of the convicted soldier for the Army and society is of equal importance.

While the determinate or fixed sentence is the rule in military law, there are a number of ways by which the military prisoner may shorten the period of confinement. They are:

First: The period of confinement may be materially decreased by good behavior, for which good conduct time is granted. This amounts to one day in six for the first year and one day in three thereafter. Thus a five-year sentence is reduced to three and one-half years by good conduct.

Second: Clemency may be granted for cogent reasons, such as meritorious acts, or on account of destitution of the prisoner's family.

Third: On the Fourth of July, Thanksgiving Day and Christmas the President of the United States pardons a certain

number prisoners upon the recommendation of the Secretary of War.

Fourth: Home parole may be granted to any prisoner after he has served one-third of his sentence, or fifteen years in the case of life imprisonment. Provided the prisoner can obtain a friend and advisor to vouch for him, and can get employment with a reliable firm, he may be paroled for the remainder of his sentence with certain restrictions as to movement and behavior.

Lastly: Any military prisoner, except those convicted of felonies, may request restoration to duty. If this request is favorably considered by a board of officers, the prisoner becomes a probationer and is enrolled in a disciplinary battalion. He sheds the prison uniform and dons the uniform of the soldier. He is given special work with periods of military instruction. After a period of probation his case is further considered and favorable action results in his restoration to duty to complete his period of enlistment. Thus, the convicted soldier is given the opportunity to reinstate himself and to escape the stigma of a dishonorable discharge.

The Pacific Branch of the United States Disciplinary Barracks is located on Alcatraz Island in San Francisco Bay. Here, on this little island, some 600 soldiers are expiating their crimes. Their sentences range from six months to life imprisonment. Approximately ten percent of them are serving sentences of ten years or more. Over one-third have been sentenced for military offenses, the remainder for misdemeanors and felonies.

The prisoners at this institution are subjected to a firm,

impartial discipline. Misconduct and misbehavior result in punishment; good conduct is rewarded. The punishments are not cruel but consist of forfeiture of good conduct time, loss of privileges, and solitary confinement for a limited period. The punishment is made to fit the offense and for minor infractions rules may be only a reprimand or the loss of one or more entertainments. Every infraction is recorded for each prisoner and this record is considered in making work assignments and in taking action on requests for parole, clemency or restoration.

All men in good standing — over 95% of the inmates of the institution — are granted all the privileges allowed by law. Such men are permitted to attend all entertainments, including motion pictures, boxing bouts, and shows provided by theatrical organizations of San Francisco and vicinity. They are permitted to write at least two letters weekly, with writing materials and stamps furnished by the government. They are issued tobacco with liberal smoking privileges. A well-stocked library is open to them. When not at work in the daytime they are allowed the freedom of the jail yard for exercise and games. Once a week all men in good standing are permitted to have visitors. Misconduct results in the loss of these privileges, from the loss of one entertainment up to the loss of all privileges for stated periods, in the most refractory cases.

The spiritual welfare of the inmates of this institution is the charge of an Army chaplain detailed for this purpose. He holds regular services, teaches Bible classes and is the friend and advisor of all. It is also his duty to provide materials for sports and to provide and supervise entertainment. His efforts are ably seconded by the Salvation Army and the Volunteers

of America. The American Red Cross and the Jewish Welfare Board co-operate by rendering assistance in such cases as destitution of relatives of prisoners.

The living conditions at Alcatraz are not uncomfortable, to say the least. The prison proper is considered to be a model in cleanliness, orderliness and sanitation. The entire 600 prisoners are housed in one great cell room, well lighted and ventilated. Each man has his own private cell, completely equipped. Every necessity is furnished him. He wears a neat black uniform. His food is that of the soldier of the United States Army, the best fed of all armies. The prisoner's laundry and dry cleaning are done for him. A sanitary barbershop and baths are open to him daily. And, finally, a well-stocked storeroom is at his service from which he draws, as needed, everything from a toothbrush to a uniform.

Every opportunity possible is afforded the ambitious man for study. Illiterates must attend school daily. For others there is a night school. Many are taking correspondence courses or devoting their evenings to self-study. The prison library has a large and varied selection of technical works. Study is encouraged to the fullest extent possible. The hours of labor, except for such men as cooks and bakers, are from 7:30 a.m. to 4:30 p.m., with one hour for the noonday meal and Saturday afternoon and Sunday off. The prisoners rise at 6:00 a.m. and go to bed at 9:00 p.m. Their work varies. Many are engaged in rock quarrying, road building, construction and farming. A large number work in the prison itself as clerks, cooks and janitors. In conformity with the mission of the institution to prepare prisoners for their return to civil life by teaching them

trades, a number of industries are operated for this purpose. A few of these industries are furniture making, tailoring, boot-making and printing. In all there are approximately fifty trades open to the ambitious prisoner.

Throughout each prisoner's period of confinement he is studied by a psychiatrist. Month after month and year after year this officer accumulates and records each man's personal history. Through correspondence and personal interview all the pertinent facts from his past, from infancy on, are unearthed. Finally, practically all of his personal history is bared and a true picture of the man obtained. All requests for parole, clemency or restoration are considered and granted or rejected in the light of this history.

Lest the picture of the prisoner's life seem too roseate let us turn to the other side of the picture. The prisoner, for long, weary months, is under a strict, never-ceasing discipline, under which every lapse brings some punishment. He is cut off from all communion with his relatives and friends, except that for one hour weekly his relatives may visit him. Day after day, night after night alluring freedom spreads itself before his eyes across the narrow waters of the bay. Narrow it may be, but a gulf to the prisoners, as some of them have discovered to their cost, in trying to escape by swimming. The city is so close that its sounds and sights are a constant reminder of the freedom that has been lost.

We have made a hasty survey of the life of the prisoners at Alcatraz. Let us now pass to that long-looked-for day — the day of the prisoner's release. He sheds at last the prison garb for tailored clothing of his own selection as to style and cloth.

His private property and funds are turned over to him. He is given a railroad ticket to his place of enlistment, or to any locality he may desire, provided the government is put to no additional expense. He is given a cash donation of $10.00. At last he is ready to go back into society. The Disciplinary Barracks have done all that can be done for him. He has led a regular life; he has had opportunity to study and to learn a trade. When he leaves the jail for the last time he is decently clothed and in no way bears the stamp of a prison. Thus prepared, his future is in his own hands."

While few prisoners were redeemed in the later years of rehabilitation while I was there, hundreds were in the early years before World War I. Even in my day the prisoners who completed their terms were discharged and sent back into society with no air of the prison about them. The prison tailors were excellent. Their shoes fit well. Their overcoat and gloves were warming. And ten bucks cash could get you through for several days during the Great Depression.

The Chaplain's View

While military leadership set the rules and the rewards and the punishments on Alcatraz, it was the Chaplain, in my opinion, who had most impact on the prisoners' lives during the five years I lived there from 1929 to 1934. He was a man to remember.

Our Chaplain was Captain Edward Sliney, a Catholic priest of Irish ancestry, assigned to the Disciplinary Barracks. It was

Chaplain Sliney with his German shepherd, "Lobo," 1930.

Chaplain Sliney who gave all those lusty young men the outlets that helped them contain the violence inherent in their young bodies.

It was Chaplain Sliney who heard their confessions and bore the ordeal of keeping them secret to himself. It was Chaplain Sliney who granted them the redeeming grace of Jesus Christ at ecumenical services.

Chaplain Sliney was the one who went by each of their cells at Christmas and gave each individual prisoner his own little hoard of Christmas goodies. And he did all these things somehow at no cost to the government.

He conducted services. He heard prisoners' worries. He counseled them. He surprised them with goodies. But that was

The cover of the fight program put together by Chaplain Sliney, one the most positive forces in prison life on Alcatraz.

just the beginning. He worked tirelessly to keep the prisoners occupied with healthy pursuits.

He was the one who had the prison theater established and kept movies coming in to show the prisoners. Most of all, he organized the boxing matches that were so popular with prisoners and guards and guests alike. The audiences grew too large for the prison arena and a few times the matches were moved to be fought at larger theaters like Fort Mason. The official programs were real keepsakes with about 40 pages to them, mostly ads procured by Chaplain Sliney so there was no cost to the government.

There were no successful escapes during our five years there. I feel part of that success was due to the efforts of Chaplain

Don't let all the officers' names fool you. Chaplain Sliney did all the work.

Sliney.

His flock was two- or three-hundred virile, husky young men, mostly in their early twenties. They were physical and inclined to violence. His big effort was to keep them under control.

He did it in many little ways, but the big way was to get them boxing. They could work out their frustrations and their hatreds and their stresses by hitting each other under Marquis of Queensbury rules.

On page 144 there is the cover sheet for one match at Fort Mason on May 5, 1930. Note the Army branch insignia; Infantry, Cavalry, Engineers, Air Corps, Signal Corps, Medical, Field Artillery and Coast Artillery, surrounding the prison bars

of Alcatraz.

In those days, to get something done in the Army two things had to happen:

Step One — You had to get the approval of the commander.
Step Two — You had to do the work yourself.

Both steps were taken by Chaplain Sliney. Major General Hines, commanding the Ninth Corps Area with headquarters at Fort Mason, approved the program. With his approval a whole bevy of officers were put to work to make it happen.

Chaplain Sliney lived in the large barracks above the dock, also called Building 64, with his two older sisters and his great dog, Lobo. I was told he sang in the shower every morning. He stayed with his parish of prisoners until the very end in June 1934.

Lobo was well mannered and friends with everyone.

Two Attempted Escapes!

Most of the prisoners were respectful of Colonel Cralle. He impressed them with his quiet courage and reasonable approach to problems. It took four years before some malcontents tried to escape again. Two of them took place in 1930 while I was there.

The first was in March 1930 when three trustees confined in the same cellblock, who worked in the blacksmith and carpenter shops, plotted for weeks to get a crowbar and some large planks. They determined they could escape through the barred window

The Sims children pet Chaplain Sliny's "Lobo" in front of Building 64, 1930.

in the barbershop using the crowbar and then escape on large wooden planks, swimming for the deserted Marin County shoreline near Sausalito.

They successfully hid in the barbershop at night, successfully crowbarred out the window, successfully ran down to the Alcatraz shore and successfully got onto their planks and set off for Sausalito.

There, their success ran out. They didn't make it. The incoming tide carried them toward Berkeley, where lots of people

lived and where they didn't want to go. It was also miles farther to the shore near Berkeley. They battled the current for nearly an hour then started shouting for help. They were freezing and drowning. After all this time, they were still so close to Alcatraz that their cries for help were heard and the prison launch took out to get them. It was night, but the Q-55's searchlight found them. They were rescued and taken back to prison. One almost died in the rough current. All three faced a general court-martial, probably lost all their Good Time and had a year added to their sentence.

Three months later, in June 1930, another trustee smeared his body with grease and set out to swim to San Francisco at night. His clothes were found on the Alcatraz shoreline, but he disappeared and his body was never recovered. There is no doubt he drowned.

There were no more escape attempts until the Feds were about to take over. Then there were a few half-hearted, nervous reactions. Marnie said they just wanted to hide and none made it to the shoreline of the island. She also said they were mostly found hiding amongst the dresses in a woman's closet in quarters on the island.

One Murder!

There was one murder of a prisoner while I was there. I have forgotten his name. Our Passmen told me about it. Two prisoners caught this one victim on the top tier of cells, grabbed him in part by the ankles and tossed him up and over the protecting rail to his splattered death on the concrete floor three

stories below. I don't believe the murderers were ever caught. As I recall, all the prisoners knew who the murderers were but none would talk to investigators. The prisoner's code applied.

I suspect there was a strong motive for the murder. The string of escapes and murders while I was there seems low to me for the number of convicts doing time.

My Own View of the Army Prisoners

I only knew a handful of the prisoners. But from them I got the sense many prisoners would rather have the security of Alcatraz in those days than be out on the streets during the Great Depression, where the unemployment rate was up to 25% and men who had been well-off or even wealthy were suddenly in a long, frosty line begging for a bite to eat.

There were a few who fought the system openly. They sometimes spent time in solitary confinement. Dad took me under the prison one day in early 1934 to view the moat of the old Citadel, which remained underneath, looking like old Spanish dungeons. He turned the lights out to show me how black it got. It was as black as any deep cavern in the world. He told me there were seldom times when he felt compelled to place prisoners down in the dark underground rooms. It was his experience that after a few days in the tomb-blackness of a dungeon with the sounds of rats scampering around, that even the most hardened of criminals decided to play ball.

Furniture for the families living on Alcatraz was often made by inmates working in the Model Industries Building and

placed in the family quarters.

There were no executions of prisoners on Alcatraz. Dad told me there was one case in the whole five years where he had a prisoner who had been sentenced for execution. He took him up to San Quentin to get the sentence carried out.

Our Own "Passmen"

When families living on Alcatraz needed servants, they hired someone from San Francisco to come over and live with them, or come over on the boat for the day and go back to San Francisco in the evening. That's the way it was for nearly 70 years until Colonel Cralle became Commandant in 1926. Soon after, he changed the arrangements for servants. He put out an order stating that no more servants would be hired. Instead, families would use prisoners for servants. To him, the aim of

Footstool made by Alcatraz prisoners in 1930.

Stan with our hosueboy, Curtis, and Ray with our cook at the time, Roney. They are sitting on the front steps of our quarters in 1930.

the Disciplinary Barracks at Alcatraz was not so much to punish as to rehabilitate. He felt the families on the island would save money because the prisoners came free; they didn't have to pay anyone.

It gave more prisoners the opportunity to become Trustees and gain limited freedom on the island. And he felt the occasional reports of theft would be stopped, that prisoners would steal less than civilian servants.

So when we got there, we were issued prisoners for servants. We did not realize it was a pretty new arrangement. I assumed it had been that way forever and thought no more about it. We did not pay them anything. They were chosen from the ranks of trustees, prisoners with good conduct. On Alcatraz, we called trustees who were household servants "Passmen." They

were authorized to leave the prison on their own in the morning, work on their own all day and report back to the prison at day's end on their own. If Marnie needed them for a dinner party at night, they would get an exemption to report back to their cell at night on their own with the help of one of the guards. Prisoners assigned to us were changed from time to time.

We had a prisoner as a cook. The one I most remember was named Egan. He was a tall, lanky dark-haired ex-soldier from Pennsylvania. He was normally self-controlled, considerate and interested in being as healthy as he could. He practiced running when he could in the prison exercise yard and was proud of his developing calf muscles. He was in prison because he had struck a non-com, or sergeant. The Army frowns on that. He was sent to Alcatraz for five years.

We had another prisoner as a houseboy. He was a short man from Rhode Island named Curtis. He talked constantly about his physical prowess. Like most of the prisoners, Curtis was a young man in his twenties.

The prisoners did tell me about things they knew and accepted. Almost all believed it was not their fault they were in prison. They told me about the seamier sides of life they had heard and experienced. They told me how they were drawn to things that were more exciting than just trying to meet their obligations. They felt no responsibility for what they did. And they really enjoyed finding ways to beat the system, whatever system it was.

Marnie had to watch out for some special things in the kitchen. Listerine could disappear because it had alcohol in it, the same for cooking sherry. Listerine had menthol and

eucalyptus in it but that didn't stop the men from drinking it to get the alcohol. Cooking sherry was full of salt but that didn't stop the prisoners from drinking it to get the alcohol. Of course, the drunken prisoner got sick, got a hangover and got a few days in an isolation cell.

There was a code of ethics amongst those prisoners, but about the only item in it was not to rat on a fellow prisoner. Their attitudes were not lost on me. One of my young accomplishments, after a lot of attempts and efforts at training, was to speak without moving my lips. The prisoners all learned to do it so the guards could not tell who was talking when they were all supposed to be silent. I got pretty good at it.

On Alcatraz, under the Disciplinary Barracks system, prisoners were not called by an assigned number, which was the practice in most other prisons. They were called instead by their last name. I don't recall ever hearing their first names. They were all former soldiers.

Lust was lurking everywhere in those young male bodies. I had it from a reliable source that the prisoners occasionally had saltpeter put in their coffee if things looked too spicy. It was supposed to cool them down. In the 1920s and 1930s on Alcatraz, everyone thought saltpeter reduced lust in males and promoted impotence. Ah, well.

Wikipedia now says saltpeter, or potassium nitrate, is used for many things. It is used as a food preservative and in fertilizer. It is used to decompose tree trunks. It is an ingredient of original gunpowder. It has been used to control hypertension and is sometimes an ingredient of toothpaste for sensitive teeth. Unfortunately, there is no scientific proof that it does any good

to control sexual feelings in male prisoners. People in the 1920s and 1930s did the best they could based on what they knew then.

The Guards

During the time I was on Alcatraz the prison guards were all soldiers in the United States Army. In the past, they had been drawn from regular units for special duty, but when I was there they had been organized into a designated prison guard company. The officer in charge was a captain who was called the Captain of the Guards. The soldiers in the prison guard company lived in a barracks that was part of Building 64 overlooking the Alcatraz dock. The building was also called the Bombproof Barracks because it had been built on the east side of the island away from the Golden Gate in a position where cannon shells from incoming enemy ships could not hit that building.

The guards had it pretty good. They had nice barracks to live in and a good mess hall. And they could get away frequently to visit San Francisco and all its wonders. I don't remember any stories of our guards getting into trouble in San Francisco. If they had, I feel the prisoners would have told me.

Some things may have been lax but others were tightly disciplined. One example was uniforms. Here are two guards leaving through the sally port for a visit to San Francisco. They were dressed for the occasion and they looked like privates to me. I'll bet the one on the right had been busted back to private from sergeant.

An Epic Exposure

An older Alcatraz boy named Dale Jones found out one young guard was known to have an enormous pecker. He told Shel and Doug and me, and of course we wanted to see. No one said anything but I'm sure our visit had the tacit permission of the 1st Sergeant. I doubt the captain ever knew. Or maybe he did. Two of the visitors were his sons.

One morning when no duty interfered, we boys were allowed to visit the endowed soldier in the barracks to see his wonder. We went to the barracks in Building 64. The quarters for the soldiers was one big room filled with soldiers' bunks,

Photo taken about 1926. That's the sally port just above the dock.
Photo courtesy of the Rod Crossley Collection.

all arranged in precise military rows. There were individual footlockers at the foot of each bunk and an individual locker for each soldier along the wall. Their rifles, 1903 Springfields, were lined up in ranks and locked up in the center of the room.

I knew they were inspected regularly by their commander, standing in front of their bunks and each wearing their parade uniforms — unless it was a special physical inspection.

There were practically no soldiers in the barracks when we arrived. That's why I felt the 1st Sergeant probably knew about our visit even though he was noticeably not there. The goal of our visit was lying on his bunk. When we were assembled, he exposed his monstrosity without a word. We didn't say a word either. That it was circumcised meant nothing to me. In those days I thought everybody came that way. Shel asked how long it was. The young soldier finally spoke. "Ten inches," he said. "At rest."

None of us had even thought of bringing a ruler to check. We accepted his word completely. Without a further word or even saying, "Thank you," we left. We were ten minutes away before anyone said anything. Wow. Goliath among the Philistines! Ten inches at rest! Never read of it in the Guinness Book of Records, but it looked huge enough to us to qualify. I wondered how a sculptor might have portrayed our experience.

12

The Feds Are Coming!

Dirty Laundry!

Little details often force big changes. "For want of a nail, etc." The Federal Bureau of Prisons was all set to take Alcatraz over in 1933. The Army intended to give it to them in 1933. All the leaders and professionals and planners on both sides signed off on it. But they all overlooked a detail.

The Army prisoners on Alcatraz were doing all the laundry for all the military posts in San Francisco. Not just the Presidio, also Fort Barry, Fort Baker, Fort Scott, Benicia Arsenal and especially Fort Mason, where the headquarters was located. There was a huge amount of laundry. When the Army posts realized this, they demanded the Alcatraz turnover be suspended until they could find someone else to handle the Army's dirty laundry.

So it took another year to work that out and find another way to do the Army's laundry. There you have the dirtiest secret of the whole transfer.

The turnover date was slipped back a year and reset for June 1934. Meantime, the Justice Department's Bureau of Federal Prisons selected its first warden, James Johnston, and began erecting guard towers and security fences that had not before existed. Their work excited the public but had no effect upon me. I continued to roam the island as I pleased. Our cook and houseboy passmen continued to report every day. Marnie continued to handle social activities and provide military information to the San Francisco Chronicle. Dad went to work every day and was the last Army officer to leave Alcatraz.

Now San Francisco stepped up to bat. They had grown used to the Army fort out in the bay. Its transformation to a prison was so gradual and quiet, the people in San Francisco accepted it and were somewhat intrigued by having a unique conversation piece so easy to view. Beside that, it had evolved from a useless clod of sandstone into a landmark that seemed not only historically important but somewhat mysterious. But an increasing part of San Francisco grew to object to the imposition of the infamous, "Devil's Island," placed by the feared Department of Justice, right in the middle of their bay. They began to yell and scream and complain. "Don't put that Devil's Island here," they shouted.

Enter the "Babe"

Anastasia Scott came in 1931 to live with her older brother and her mother. They lived right behind Sergeant Thornton and his family on the little hill that stuck out into the parade ground. Anastasia was a slim, athletic, personable girl of seventeen who seemed mature beyond her years. She was always most pleasant with me and treated me as an equal. She had a quiet, likeable voice. We seemed to be comfortable with each other and often chatted about little things. She was always very supportive of me.

To show our admiration for her prowess we called her "Babe," after Babe Didrikson who was the outstanding female athlete of those times. She became Babe Scott.

Babe was a natural born leader. She was an immediate hit at Galileo High School and quickly became President of the Girls Athletic Association, which had more than 2,000 members. She was also selected for the staff of the excellent Galileo annual called the "Telescope." She led the girls' swimming team to championship after championship. She was a very big persona in a high school with a huge student body. She excelled in swimming and had aspirations of becoming an Olympic star. She graduated from Galileo with the Class of June 1933.

Then she had the idea of swimming from Alcatraz to San Francisco. She was a dedicated performer and set to work in secret to get ready.

Six months later, on the morning of October 17, 1933, she slipped into the cold, choppy waters of the San Francisco Bay and swam on her own from Alcatraz to the Dolphin Swimming

Club Dock on the shores of San Francisco at the foot of Van Ness Avenue. Newspaper articles say she made the mile and some swim in 43 minutes. The newspapers and the radios had a field day. Even without TV, they made quite a splash.

San Francisco didn't want a "Devil's Island" in their bay. Their position was if a slip of a girl could swim away from Alcatraz, anyone could do it. The opposition to a "Devil's Island" in San Francisco Bay mushroomed like an explosion of dynamite. Everybody chimed in! Hundreds of national articles were written about her. She was hounded for her own story dozens of times.

For two weeks she became a national celebrity. She had done what no other woman had ever done. She had successfully swum in the cold and treacherous waters of San Francisco Bay, against the merciless tides and chill that had killed so many men. She was the first to swim from infamous Alcatraz to the freedom shores of San Francisco.

Anastasia "Babe" Scott, in the Galileo High School's "Telescope," their annual, published in 1933.

Well, all that hullabaloo made no difference to the Federal Bureau of Prisons or the Department of Justice. They went right ahead with their plans to take over The Rock and fill it with the nation's worst criminals.

What I remember most about this event, and the memory remains vivid to this day, was that in all that newspaper and radio attention, in all those hundreds of news articles, no one ever said much about the facts that:

1.   *Babe waited for months to find the right moment, with tides at a standstill, to begin her swim.*

2.   *She was all coated up with grease, like the women who swam the English Channel.*

3.   *She had a boat with her all the way, with two men from the Dolphin Club aboard and a well-known local woman swimmer named Edna Curry.*

4.   *The men in the boat kept steering her. That's critical.*

5.   *She was a champion swimmer with the Western Womens Athletic Club.*

Babe Scott's life was all downhill from then on. The media overwhelmed her. She left Alcatraz not the victim of prisoners, but of a media feeding frenzy.

You know what? That influenced my feelings about the media ever since. I have never forgiven them. Those I have tried to talk to about it never expressed one word of responsibility for what the media did to "Babe" Scott.

The Last Army Prisoners

With the transfer looming, the Army stopped sending new prisoners in to Alcatraz. Some finished their terms and departed in their new suit and with their 10 dollars cash. When we left the island in June 1934, there were a few Army prisoners still there. They were felt to be the worst we had. Long timers. Some for 20 years. One for Life.

Of the 32 Army prisoners left to the mercies of the Federal penitentiary, the leading crime was robbery, followed closely by sodomy! Sodomy was a major, major crime to the Army in those days.

The top historian in my opinion on old Fort Alcatraz is John Martini, former Park Service Ranger on Alcatraz. He kindly provided a copy of the order terminating our quarters on Alcatraz. It was probably the last order published by the Disciplinary Barracks and told us to be out of our Alcatraz home on June 21, 1934. That meant Dad and Marnie and Ray and Stan and I probably departed from Alcatraz on June 21, 1934, exactly five years to the day from when we arrived at Fort Mason in 1929.

Honorary Wardens

When the Federal Bureau of Persons took over Alcatraz, the Assistant Director of the Bureau was James V. Bennett. He was probably more intimately involved with the turnover of Alcatraz to the Feds than any other single official. He became the Director in 1937 and remained in that post until 1964, a tenure

longer than any other Director in the history of the Federal Bureau of Prisons.

I did not meet him then, but in 1968 I designed a certificate naming Dad and Marnie as Honorary Wardens of Alcatraz. I wanted something special to give them on their 50th wedding anniversary. He had been Warden Johnston's boss when the Feds took over Alcatraz in 1934. He was still the boss during the Alcatraz riot in 1945.

I sent it to Mr. Bennett asking him to sign it. It turned out he had been impressed with the concept of convict rehabilitation

James V. Bennett, about 1967.

used at the Disciplinary Barracks on Alcatraz and had applied some of those principles to the Federal Bureau of Prisons when he set up their Minimum Security Prisons.

He was retired from the Bureau in 1968, but signed the certificate as the President of the Joint Commission on Correctional Manpower and Training.

The certificate I designed naming Dad and Marnie as Honorary Wardens of Alcatraz.

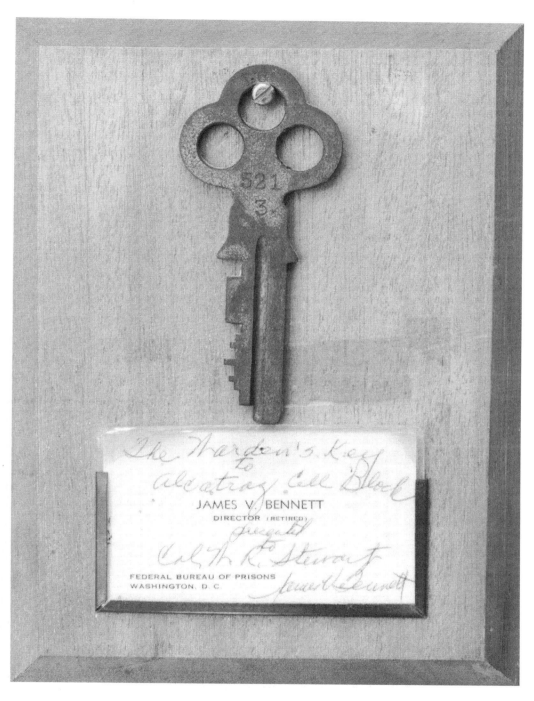

The certificate and the key are currently in my custody.

Summary

In summary, let me say I was in daily contact with Army prisoners throughout the five years I lived on Alcatraz. My young character was such that I soaked up the prisoners' attitudes like a sponge.

It took years of family help and military training to get me to reverse my attitudes and start taking responsibility for what I did with my life.

One little thing I realized on my own is that I began to feel my conduct as a teenager had been such that I was in a poor position to be critical of others. I have tried to keep that humbling realization close with me throughout the years and avoid criticizing anyone.

It took years to begin to comprehend the wisdom of Albert Einstein when he said, "A life of service to others is a life that is worthwhile!"

Epilogue

My father and mother were great Americans. Dad was always ready for good fellowship. He had a talent for leading men. His career as an Army officer was exemplary and his mastery of the English language was a wonder to behold. Marnie was an outstanding practitioner of the social graces and was talented in music and literature. Together they raised three sons. I honor them biblically and personally.

But the paths taken by offspring are often strange and difficult to comprehend. By the time my family left Alcatraz, I was a candidate for judicial attention. Fortunately for me, family closed in and began my redemption the following year. Dad and Marnie wisely sent me to live with my grandparents and an aunt and uncle when I was sixteen. My grandparents were inspiring personalities and my aunt and uncle spent their nights trying to stay two weeks ahead of me and encourage me to get interested in the right activities. I didn't even realize how well they did it until many years later. It was with them that my turnaround began.

Family is the first line of defense to maintain social standards and feelings about right and wrong. It would take many years for a sense of right and wrong to set in for me, but that is when it began. My humble gratitude goes to my family, everyone. God bless us all!

San Antonio, TX

Thank You!

I would like to credit Joshua Bennett Winer and Joshua Pelletier with plowing through my manuscript, word by word, and doing an outstanding job of correcting my mistakes of grammar and punctuation. They both tell periods where to go and duel with every comma. In a day when our society is throwing away all the rules for written communication, they remain reviewers with high standards. Thank you to both Joshes.

The book cover was designed by Lauren V. Allen whose creative talent finds symbols of expression for the meats of thought behind the sauce of words and attractive ways to present them. Hers is a skill that is invaluable to any author. Lauren, my sincere congratulations.

The project director and my agent has been Mackenzie Smith of Mackannecheese Media. She exhibits a marvelous combination of insistence, consideration, persistence and forgiveness that was just what the doctor ordered for me. Alcatraz Kid would never be published without her. Sustained applause, Mack! Thank you!

I recommend without reservation this fine young team from Austin, Texas.

2017

Photo Credits

Salute

The crest of the Class of January 1943, used with permission by the West Point Class of January, 1943.

Introduction

Golden Gate National Recreation Area. Photo by Jennifer Wan, purchased from Shutterstock on October 18, 2017. https://www.shutterstock.com/image-photo/panorama-pacific-ocean-golden-gate-bridge-671045071

Century Plants, photo by Noelle Johnson, the AZ Plant Lady. Used with her permission. https://www.azplantlady.com/2016/04/california-road-trip-day-8-gardens-of.html

Chapter 1

General Robert Callahan, The Coast Artillery Journal, 1924 via wikipedia: https://en.wikipedia.org/wiki/Robert_Emmet_Callan.

Chateau Thierry, http://www.navsource.org/archives/09/22/22031.html, via Mike Green.

Hotel Richelieu, picture of a postcard, purchased from

cardcow.com.

The Q-55, The Alcatraz Launch, Courtesy of the Sims Family.

Pier 4, source unknown.

The PX, Photo courtesy of Alcatraz Alumni, via John Brunner. alcatrazalumni.org.

Chapter 2

Modern Coastline Map via www.dot.ca.gov/dist4/yerba-buena/aybi_geology.

Captain William H. Warner. The portrait was made available courtesy of Anchor Books of Chico and descending cousin Phil Warner.

Major Zealous B. Tower via wikipedia, photographer unknown. https://en.wikipedia.org/wiki/Zealous_Bates_Tower

Major General James B. McPherson. via wikipedia, photographer unknown. https://en.wikipedia.org/wiki/James_B._McPherson

Lt. Col. Joseph Stewart. Photo from the West Point Library. The Memorial Article of the Annual Review of the Associations of Graduates, June 13th, 1905. Student Number 1128.

Chapter 3

Alcatraz in 1930, photographer unknown. Photo sourced from Alcatraz Alumni via John Brunner. alcatrazalumni.org.

Dad, Bob, Grandpa, Stanley, Marnie and Ray in 1933. Stewart family photo.

Lennie Sims. Courtesy of the Sims family.
Well-dressed Infantry captain. Courtesy of the Sims family.

Seagulls. Photo courtesy of Alcatraz Alumni, via John
Brunner. alcatrazalumni.org.

Chapter 4

Capt. and Mrs. W. R. Stewart in 1918. Family photo.
Little Marnie. Stewart family photo.
1924 Mary Agnes Stewart. Stewart family photo.
Captain W. R Stewart in 1917. Stewart family photo. The
Indiana, via wikipedia, photographer unknown.
https://en.wikipedia.org/wiki/SS_Indiana_(1873)
David & Mary Jane Stewart in Pittsburgh. Stewart family
photo.
Dad with Ray and Stan in 1930. Stewart family photo.
Brothers Three. Stewart family photo.
Ray in the summer of 1929. Stewart family photo.
Ray in 1931. Stewart family photo.
Stanley in 1930. Stewart family photo.
BG Raymond F. Metcalfe (MC)
Easter 1932. Stewart family photo.
1931 Stanley on Top. Stewart family photo.
Stanley Salutes. Taken from Rotogravure Society Section
of the San Francisco Chronicle in 1933. Stewart family photo.
Three Young Stewarts. Stewart family photo.
Bobby, age 10. Stewart family photo.
We three boys at Fort MacArthur in 1934. Stewart family photo.

Chapter 5

1930, Last Ride Of The "Hack." Courtesy of the Sims family.
School Essay Forward. Stewart family records.
Eighth grade class picture at Grant School in San Fransisco.
Stewart family photo.

Chapter 6

Colonel George H. Mendell in about 1885, via the historical Army Foundation. https://armyhistory.org/company-a-u-s-engineer-battalion-june-1864-one-of-the-most-brilliant-scenes-of-the-war/

1876 Later Excavating Stage of South Face. Photograph by Edward Muybridge. Used with permission from the Bancroft Library, University of California.

1924 view from the Parade Ground. San Francisco History Center, San Francisco Public Library.

Chapter 7

Books. Stewart Family Photo.

The Graf Zepplin. Photo courtesy of the Sims family.

Mining Harbors and Bays. USAT Minelayer photo in
1933. US Army photo, photographer unknown.

1932 Doug Thompson, Bobby Stewart and Sheldon Thompson, Family Photo.

Chapter 8

The LaSalle. Stephen J. Brown, Bo Bell and the Barrett Jackson Showroom in Scottsdale, AZ.

Ray, Bobbie and Stanley by the Fort Mason garage in 1932. Stewart family photo.

Grandpa Ray Simpson and Bobby Stewart August 1929. Stewart family photo.

Dr. Abigail Winegar Simpson. Stewart family photo.

Ten Cents a Dance. © 1931, renewed 1958 Columbia Pictures Industries, Inc. All Rights Reserved. Courtesy of Columbia Pictures.

Chapter 9

The Major General Frank M. Coxe. Photo courtesy of Alcatraz Alumni, via John Brunner. http://www.alcatrazalumni.org/BOATS/GENERAL%20COXE%20%20L.jpg.

Jean Parker. Photo by Otto Dyar via Wikimedia Commons. https://commons.wikimedia.org/wiki/File:Jean_Parker_-_still.jpg.

Chapter 10

Major Rueben B. Turner about 1895. The USMA Library Archives.

Chapter 11

Captain G. Maury Cralle, USMA 1896. Courtesy of Ret. Colonel Cralle's Grandson, LTC Maury S. Cralle, Jr., USMA 1956.

1933 Major W.R. Stewart family photo.

Lobo. Courtesy of the Sims family.

Alcatraz Fights. Copy of the first page of the 1930 Fight Program.

Sims with Lobo. Courtesy of the Sims family.

Footstool. Photo by Mackenzie Smith.

Stan with our houseboy, Curtis, and Ray with our cook. Stewart family photo.

Two Soldiers at the sally port, photo courtesy of The Rod Crossley Collection.

Chapter 12

Babe Scott. Photo from 1932 Galileo High School Yearbook.

Honorary warden certificate. Photo by author.

Master cell block key. Stewart family photo.

10031623R00107

Made in the USA
Lexington, KY
17 September 2018